KT-453-576

God's Chosen People

*A Theological Interpretation of the
Book of Deuteronomy*

R. E. CLEMENTS

SCM PRESS LTD
BLOOMSBURY STREET LONDON

334 – 00561 – 2

First published 1968

© *SCM Press Ltd 1968*

Printed in Great Britain by
Billing & Sons Limited
Guildford and London

GOD'S CHOSEN PEOPLE

CONTENTS

5

Contents

ABBREVIATIONS

ATANT	Abhandlungen zur Theologie des Alten und Neuen Testaments
BA	*The Biblical Archaeologist*
BWANT	Beiträge zur Wissenschaft vom Alten und Neuen Testament
BZ	*Biblische Zeitschrift*
CBQ	*Catholic Biblical Quarterly*
E	Elohist Source
FRLANT	Forschungen zur Religion und Literatur des Alten und Neuen Testaments
IB	*The Interpreter's Bible*
IDB	*The Interpreter's Dictionary of the Bible*
J	Yahwist Source
JBL	*Journal of Biblical Literature*
P	Priestly Source
RB	*Revue biblique*
SBS	Stuttgarter Bibelstudien
SBT	Studies in Biblical Theology
ThLZ	*Theologische Literaturzeitung*
VT	*Vetus Testamentum*
WMANT	Wissenschaftliche Monographien zum Alten und Neuen Testament
ZAW	*Zeitschrift für die alttestamentliche Wissenschaft*

ABBREVIATIONS

I

THE SIGNIFICANCE OF THE BOOK OF DEUTERONOMY

WITHIN the modern study of the Old Testament the book of Deuteronomy has come to enjoy a place of special importance, and has received a considerable amount of attention from biblical scholars. There are a number of reasons for this, not the least of which is the particular attractiveness and interest of the teaching which it contains. Both for its theological and for its historical significance it stands out among the writings of the Pentateuch, and provides a valuable insight into the Israelite conception and use of law. Furthermore it has a special importance for the study of the Old Testament as a canon of sacred scripture because its appearance marked the beginning of that process which eventually led to the collection and formation of a special canon of authoritative writings. Therefore, in these three aspects, theological, historical and canonical, the book of Deuteronomy has a particular significance, and provides an instructive guide to the religious meaning of the Old Testament.

Deuteronomy as a Theological Document

In order to appreciate why Deuteronomy is particularly important theologically we must reconsider
carefully the place and function of theology in religion.
Theology is concerned with religious ideas, and with
the element of meaning in religious acts; as such it is
simply a part of the much wider experience and practice of religion. When a modern Christian enters a
church, and participates in the sacrament of Holy
Communion, he is aware that this is a religious act
which has a special meaning for him, and he naturally
attaches a great deal of importance to this. He will
probably be aware that other Christians interpret it
rather differently from himself, even though they are
agreed as to the importance of the basic rite. It is with
these questions of the significance and interpretation
of religious acts that theology is concerned. It arises out
of reflection upon the experiences which people
undergo, and the sacred acts which they perform.

In the modern western world, particularly under
the influence of the Judaeo-Christian tradition, the
theological element in religion is given very considerable emphasis, and a great deal of religious energy is
expended upon the communication of theological
ideas. In the long history of religion, however, this has
not usually been the case, and the theological and
intellectual aspects of religion have not always been
given very great prominence. The broader demands
of worship and devotion have been met without any
great attention to their intellectual justification. The
simple assertions of historical precedent and practical
necessity have been sufficient to guarantee the con-

tinuing performance of religious acts through many generations. This does not mean that these acts have been performed unintelligently, or without any adequate sense of purpose, but that their interpretation has been of the simplest kind, and little effort has been made to relate these interpretations to other realms of knowledge. Religious thinking has predominantly been of a symbolic nature, and religious institutions have usually made very considerable use of visual and verbal symbolism. It is clear that many religions have survived, and have profoundly influenced the lives of people, without very much theology. Even today this is still true of certain religious traditions where institutions and symbols are of far greater importance than any systematic presentation of religious ideas.

An acquaintance with the religion of ancient Israel, as we know it through the pages of the Old Testament, shows that it was at first a predominantly cultic religion, which centred upon public worship at certain recognized institutions, of which the most important one was the Jerusalem temple. It was only gradually that Israel developed a deep interest in the reflective and interpretative aspects of its faith. The process of developing a theology as an interpretation of its religion was only slowly advanced, and Israel never, in the Old Testament period, reached the point of composing a creed to summarize its beliefs about God and the nature and destiny of man, still less of producing a systematic account of the doctrines of its faith. It would be very much easier for us today to write an Old Testament theology if Israel had done either of these things, but we must recognize Israel's religion for what it was, and not project back into it an orderliness of theological expression which it did not possess. However, although Israel never produced a creed it was certainly not lacking in theological concern, and it strove very ardently to provide an interpretation of its faith. From a very early period we find theological questions being raised in connection with the cult, and it was the need to explain and interpret the rites of worship which provided one of the fundamental impulses towards theological thinking in Israel.[1] The need for theological explanation was an important factor in the making of the Old Testament, and led Israel to differentiate itself sharply from its neighbours, even in the interpretation of religious rites which they held in common.

It is in the growing development of a reflective and theological interest in Israel's religion that the book of Deuteronomy has a special place. It appeared as an attempt to provide an interpretation of that religion, and to show why certain rites should be performed and why Israel stood in a special relationship to God. Most particularly it was concerned to show the nature and character of God, and the ways in which men and women in Israel could enjoy communion with him. Inevitably it had to adopt a polemical attitude over a number of issues in order to remove from Israel what it considered to be false religious thinking, and to cut off those sources from which such false thinking sprang. It clearly recognized that a wide variety, not to say confusion, of religious beliefs and practices were current in Israel, producing a good deal of social unrest

[1] Cf. Ex. 12.26 and 13.14, where Israelite children are prompted to raise the question 'What do you mean by this service?' in connection with the celebration of Passover.

and leading to a most damaging moral decline. The authors of Deuteronomy were concerned to stiffen the mental and moral fibres of Israel's citizens by providing them with a new, and clearer, understanding of God, and of the unique relationship which bound them to him. They endeavoured to reawaken the religious sensitivities of Israelite men, women and children, and to give them a firmer grasp of what their religion was about. Deuteronomy represents a very early, and a remarkably comprehensive, attempt at reforming religion by a programme of religious education in which every person was to be included, from the king as the head of the nation to every child in every home.[2] Both the practical, as well as the more strictly intellectual, aspects of this theological instruction become evident in Deuteronomy, so that it can be seen to belong to a very determined endeavour to strengthen and purify Israel's faith by explaining its meaning and purpose.

Together with this polemical and reforming interest in Deuteronomy we can see an essentially popular aim. Its teaching was directed to the whole nation, and not simply to one group or class of its members. This is shown by the literary character and style of Deuteronomy. The central part of the book is a code of laws contained in chapters 12-26. This is given a long introduction by a series of historical narratives and exhortations in chapters 1-11, while the remaining chapters, 27-31, provide general warnings and promises, followed by two poems in chapters 32-3,

[2] The emphasis upon the instruction of children is a striking feature of Deuteronomy. Cf. Deut. 4.9, 10; 6.7, 20; 11.19; 31.13; 32.7, 46.

with a historical epilogue in chapter 34. The central code can be seen to follow in part the collection of laws found in an earlier Israelite legal document, the Book of the Covenant (Ex. 20.22-23.19), which dates back to a very early age, perhaps c. 1200 B.C., and provides the earliest extensive presentation of Israelite civil law. It was a manual of legal practice compiled for the guidance of judges concerned with the administration of law. Deuteronomy on the other hand is essentially a popular book, and was intended to reach the ears of every man, woman and child in the nation:

And these words which I command you this day shall be upon your heart; and you shall teach them diligently to your children, and shall talk of them when you sit in your house, and when you walk by the way, and when you lie down, and when you rise. And you shall bind them as a sign upon your hand, and they shall be as frontlets between your eyes. And you shall write them on the doorposts of your house and on your gates (Deut. 6.5-9).

At least a part of the introductory section belonged to the earliest edition of Deuteronomy, and most recent Old Testament scholars have seen its commencement in 4.44-5:

This is the law which Moses set before the children of Israel; these are the testimonies, the statutes and the ordinances, which Moses spoke to the children of Israel when they came out of Egypt (Deut. 4.44-5).

The chapters and verses which precede this introduction have been variously explained. Wide acceptance has been accorded to the view of M. Noth, that chapters 1-3 were intended as an introduction to the

14

Deuteronomistic History (Deut.–II Kings),[3] and G. E. Wright has argued that all, or most, of 4.1-43 also belong to this.[4] It is probable that chapter 28 belonged to the original Deuteronomy, but that some of the material within 4.44–26.19 has been added later.[5]

A great importance attaches to the recognition of the extent of the original Deuteronomy, since this shows that the hortatory preaching style of the introductory speeches, which also reappears in the law code, is the essential style of the Deuteronomists. Its origin is not in the cold and formal pronouncements of a judge, but in the passionate preaching of religious ministers. G. von Rad has summed it up splendidly in saying 'It is preached law'.[6] Its model is the sermon, not the statute book.

This Deuteronomic style is so distinctive that it is the most easily recognizable in the whole Old Testament. It is marked by comparatively long sentences, a favourite vocabulary, the frequent use of synonyms, and a passionate fullness of exhortation which clearly

[3] M. Noth, Überlieferungsgeschichtliche Studien I, rep. Tübingen, 1957, pp. 25 f.

[4] Wright, 'Deuteronomy', *IB*, II, 1953, pp. 316, 351.

[5] G. Minette de Tillesse, 'Sections "tu" et sections "vous" dans le Deutéronome', *VT* 12, 1962, pp. 29-87, has argued that these later additions can be recognized by their use of the plural form, and that they are the work of the Deuteronomistic Historian.

[6] G. von Rad, *Studies in Deuteronomy* (SBT 9), London, 1953, p. 16. Cf. the same author's comment in 'The Levitical Sermon in I and II Chronicles', *The Problem of the Hexateuch and Other Essays*, Edinburgh, 1966, p. 267, 'Deuteronomy is motivated by a desire to instruct such as we find in no other book of the Old Testament'.

mark out its authors as preachers rather than lawyers. It is directed towards moving the minds and wills of men, and we cannot doubt that this style arose in sermons exhorting Israel to be loyal to Yahweh rather than in the precision of a legal handbook. A prominent feature of this style is its use of the 'I–Thou' mode of address, and the whole book, including its central law code, is cast in the form of a speech given by Moses to Israel in the plains of Moab before its entry into Canaan. This style, therefore, is wholly in keeping with the general character of Deuteronomy as a work intended for religious instruction and education. By recounting history, by reiterating ancient laws, and by exhorting Israel to a right way of thinking and acting, Deuteronomy strives after a maximum theological grasp of its faith, and an effective deepening of Israel's religious understanding. It is one of the most consistently theological writings of the whole Old Testament.

The way in which Deuteronomy describes its contents is therefore worthy of attention. It is said to be 'law' (Hebrew, *tōrāh*),[7] which originally referred not to law in the juridical sense, but to religious instruction such as was normally given by a priest, and which could also describe the teaching of a prophet or a wise man.[8] This *tōrāh* is defined more precisely by Deuteronomy as 'testimonies, statutes and ordinances',[9] which

[7] Deut. 4.44; 17.18f.; cf. 31.9.

[8] See G. Östborn, *Tōrā in the Old Testament. A Semantic Study*, Lund, 1945, pp. 89 ff. R. Rendtorff, 'Tora', *RGG*[3], VI, cols. 950 f.

[9] Deut. 4.45; cf. Deut. 12.1 where the following materials are described as 'statutes and ordinances'.

are more specifically legal terms.[10] There is in Deuteronomy, therefore, a close identification of legal statutes with religious instruction, which is significant in view of later developments in Judaism. The basis of this identification of law with religious instruction goes back to the Elohistic tradition of the Sinai covenant, which asserted that the Decalogue (Ex. 20.2-17), and the Book of the Covenant represented the legal requirements of the covenant between God and Israel. The administration of law was thus brought under the authority of religion in a remarkably close way, and the description which Deuteronomy gives to its contents is derived from its relationship to the Horeb (Sinai) covenant.[11] It contains law, but it is not law in a strictly juridical sense, since its purpose is religious instruction and edification.

Many of the regulations set out by Deuteronomy were not new, or were only relatively new in their detailed requirements. What was remarkably new in Israel was such a thoroughgoing attempt at providing everyone with an interpretation of the meaning and obligations of its religion. Israel was being taught to worship God with its understanding, as well as with its heart. In consequence of this we find that great stress is laid upon the attitude which was to be adopted towards God, and towards the public service of him

[10] For the legal setting of 'ordinances' (Heb. *mišpāṭîm*) see A. Alt, 'The Origins of Israelite Law', *Essays on Old Testament History and Religion*, Oxford, 1966, pp. 92, 123 f. For 'Statutes' (Heb. *ḥuqqîm*) see R. Hentschke, *Satzung und Setzender. Ein Beitrag zur israelitischen Rechtsterminologie* (BWANT V : 3), Stuttgart, 1963, pp. 28.

[11] Horeb is the name by which the book of Deuteronomy refers to the mountain otherwise known as Sinai.

in worship. Similarly we find exhortations regarding the attitude that was to be nurtured in thinking of one's fellow countrymen, and of others resident in the land. Not only what ought to be done, but in what spirit it ought to be done, became important matters of principle. We have, therefore, in Deuteronomy a very important step along the road which led to the recognition that 'God is spirit, and those who worship him must worship in spirit and truth' (John 4.24). Thus the book of Deuteronomy has a special claim to attention in the study of Old Testament theology because of the emphasis which it places upon Israel's own religious understanding.

Deuteronomy and Josiah's Reformation

There is also a great historical interest in Deuteronomy, which arises from the fact that a major part of it was concerned in a reform which took place in Jerusalem in the reign of king Josiah in 621 B.C.[12] This knowledge may at first glance seem a limited asset since we do not know precisely how much of Deuteronomy was available to Josiah, nor do we know how long before his reign the book was written. Nevertheless the importance of the connection of Deuteronomy with Josiah's reform is considerable.

In the first place we have a very valuable fixed point in relating the development of the traditions which make up our present Pentateuch to the actual course of Israel's religious development. It is seldom possible to define with any precision the point at which extant documents emerged in Israel, yet it is a convincing

[12] This is described in II Kings 22.3 ff.

contention of scholarship that an earlier edition of Deuteronomy was the law book which was found in the Jerusalem temple in Josiah's time and which gave a new direction to its worship. Thus we are in a position to relate the chronological sequence of traditions in the Pentateuch to at least one major event in Israel's religious life.

There is, however, a further great advantage accruing from the identification of an edition of Deuteronomy with Josiah's law book. The discovery of this book led to a large scale reform of worship which exalted Jerusalem to become the sole sanctuary at which it was legitimate for Israelites and Jews to offer sacrifice to Yahweh. The later significance of Jerusalem as the centre of orthodox Judaism was in a measure the result of Josiah's action. Yet it seems certain that Deuteronomy grew up on the basis of traditions which did not originate from Jerusalem, at least not from its priesthood. This fact can be deduced from a comparison of the teaching regarding the cult in Deuteronomy with the teaching that we know represents the Jerusalem tradition. This latter can be seen reflected in other literary works of the Old Testament, especially the Holiness Code, the Restoration Programme of Ezekiel (Ezek. 40-8), and the Priestly Document. It is also quite noticeable, although in a rather different way, in the prophecies of Isaiah, Ezekiel and Deutero-Isaiah. This cultic tradition of Jerusalem must have grown up, and been preserved, among the Zadokite priests, who, since Solomon's time, had provided the official priests of the Jerusalem temple.[13] It is impossible to explain the cultic traditions of

[13] Cf. I Kings 2.35.

19

Deuteronomy as a natural development of the Jerusalem (Zadokite) tradition. Whence then did they
originate?

Since the suggestion was first made by C. F. Burney,
it has become a widely held view that the traditions
upon which Deuteronomy was based arose in the
Northern Kingdom of Israel.[14] They have been especially linked with the shrines of Shechem and Bethel,
and some of them have been thought ultimately to go
back to the old amphictyony of tribes of the pre-
monarchic era. This latter claim would certainly be
contested, but it has some justification. This conclusion
regarding the northern origin of the traditions behind
Deuteronomy does not mean that the book was actually
composed in the North. There are many difficulties
which adhere to such a view. In the first place this
kingdom had been incorporated into the Assyrian
empire since the downfall of Samaria in 721 B.C., and
its cultic life had been severely disrupted. There is
also much in Deuteronomy which points to a familiarity with, and concern for, the political and cultic
traditions of Jerusalem.[15] The final composition of
Deuteronomy must certainly have been accomplished
in the capital of Judah. Nevertheless Josiah's reform

[14] C. F. Burney, *The Book of Judges*, London, 1918, p. xlvi
note. It has found much support, particularly in the writings of
A. C. Welch and G. von Rad. See A. C. Welch, *The Code of
Deuteronomy. A New Theory of Its Origin*, London, 1923, and
G. von Rad, *Deuteronomy. A Commentary*, London, 1966. It is
also accepted by G. E. Wright in 'Deuteronomy' *IB*, II, 1953,
pp. 309-537.

[15] I have endeavoured to show this in my article 'Deuteronomy and the Jerusalem Cult Tradition', *VT* 15, 1965, pp.
300-12.

witnessed the adoption and enforcement in Jerusalem of traditions which derived from outside this city.

No aspect of the comparison between the Deuteronomic teaching and the older Jerusalem traditions is more interesting than that which concerns the kingship. Deuteronomy is unique among Israel's law books in its inclusion of a law regarding the kingship,[16] which particularly points out that the king is an ordinary Israelite, who has been chosen by the people and God for a special administrative task. Further, in the account of Josiah's reformation, the prophetess Huldah is said to have praised Josiah because by his action he had 'humbled himself before the Lord'.[17] The king's own submission to the demands of the law is thus given a central place. All of this contrasts very markedly with the exalted view of the kingship which was current in Jerusalem, and which regarded the Davidic monarch as uniquely God's 'son'.[18] Josiah's action undoubtedly meant that he submitted to a view of the monarchy which was very much less pretentious than the older royal ideology which we see reflected in certain psalms. Deuteronomy can therefore be seen as a striking new development in the religious estimate of the role of the monarchy in Israel. We shall also see that this is reflected in the Deuteronomic interpretation of the covenant between Yahweh and Israel. All of this bears out our contention that Deuteronomy has a distinctive historical importance for the light which it sheds on the growth of Israel's religious and political institutions.

[16] Deut. 17.14-20.
[17] II Kings 22.19.
[18] Cf. especially Pss. 2.7; 89.26; II Sam. 7.14.

This particular background to Deuteronomy prompts us to ask who its authors might have been. Its lofty moral earnestness and its deeply spiritual tone have led many writers to see it as a development of the preaching of the great eighth-century prophets.[19] There are difficulties attaching to this view, however, which has resulted in many scholars discarding it in favour of the view that the authors must have been more closely attached to the cult and the priesthood. Thus they must have been Levites,[20] since Deuteronomy regards these as the legitimate priests of Israel, although it is not necessary to conclude that they were all still practising priestly duties at the time when they composed this work. They appear to have regarded their task as a teaching one primarily, and their service of the altar as subordinate to this. If their true home lay in the Northern Kingdom, it is reasonable to conclude that they had either abandoned, or been expelled from, their sanctuaries in the North. After the Assyrian conquest and annexation of Northern Israel in 721 B.C., they had moved south and settled in the cities and villages of Judah. That the Deuteronomists were to be found among such Levites is the presupposition of the present study. Such a conclusion

[19] For a recent statement of the view that a prophetic party was the source of Deuteronomy see E. W. Nicholson, *Deuteronomy and Tradition*, Oxford, 1967, pp. 73 ff., 117 f., 122.

[20] This is particularly argued by G. von Rad, *Studies in Deuteronomy*, pp. 66 ff.; *Deuteronomy. A Commentary*, pp. 24 ff. G. E. Wright, 'Deuteronomy', pp. 325 f. It is also advocated by A. Bentzen, *Die josianische Reform und ihre Voraussetzungen*, Copenhagen, 1926, pp. 64 ff. Cf. also P. Buis and J. Leclerc, *Le Deutéronome*, Paris, 1963, pp. 15 f.

reveals an important aspect of the work of Israel's priesthood which has often been neglected.[21]

Deuteronomy and the Canon

The book of Deuteronomy also possesses a great interest for the study of the origin of the canon of the Old Testament. The word 'canon' meant a measuring rod, and when it came to be applied to the writings of the Old Testament it denoted those books which Jews, and subsequently Christians, regarded as authoritative documents of their faith. While many parts of the present Old Testament go back to a very great antiquity, so that even substantial documents which are now incorporated in it may have been written as far back as Solomon's age, these documents were not at first intended to be canonical in the later sense. It was later generations of Jews which came to regard these writings as of special religious importance which marked them out from other literature. Just as St Paul was not intending to write canonical scriptures when he wrote his epistles, so many of the original authors of the histories and psalms of the Old Testament would have been surprised that later generations attached such a unique authority to their work. The origin of the Old Testament canon is an obscure process, in which only some of the important milestones are clear. While the religions of the peoples surrounding Israel also had sacred writings and psalms, none of them produced a canon of these writings, or placed as great an emphasis upon their preservation as did Israel. Of all the many remarkable aspects of the Israelite-

[21] Cf. Deut. 33.10.

Jewish faith none is more distinctive than the collecting and handing on of its sacred scriptures, and no material objects have been deemed by Jews more worthy of the adjective 'holy' than the scrolls and books which contain them. The Old Testament is the written testimony to Israel's belief in its election. We may well ask how this all began, and when Israel first began to establish a canon of scriptures as the yardstick of its faith and conduct.

In the making of a canon of the Old Testament the role played by the book of Deuteronomy in Josiah's reform has been widely regarded as an important first step.[22] With the acceptance of the Deuteronomic laws as binding upon all Israel a great change began to take place in the nation's religion, and a written document became an authoritative rule for the conduct of its national life. Thereafter the canonical principle was firmly established, and other writings were added to make a code of instruction for future generations of Jews. Thus Deuteronomy has a special place in the study of the Old Testament canon, not simply because it is a part of it, but because its own appearance in Josiah's reform provides us with an insight into the process which made such a canon important. From the relationship of Deuteronomy with this event we can learn some of the reasons which prompted the regulation of religious and national life by a sacred book, and we can discover the kind of authority which it was believed to possess. It has been claimed that the book of Deuteronomy was 'canonized' by Josiah in 621

[22] Cf. R. H. Pfeiffer, 'Canon of the OT', *IDB*, I, pp. 502 f. G. von Rad, *O.T. Theology*, II, Edinburgh and London, 1965, p. 395.

B.C.,[23] but this is to use the language of a later age for an action which did not primarily intend to establish, or define, a collection of sacred scriptures. Josiah was not intending to achieve the same kind of result as was sought by the later Jewish leaders who accepted and defined the canonical status of the Old Testament. Indeed Josiah was in no way seeking to confer a particular authority upon the law book which was found in the temple, but rather to act in a way commensurate with the authority which its demands possessed. This led to what may be termed a canonical cult as much as a canonical book, since the centralization of worship at Jerusalem was inseparable from the reverence accorded to Deuteronomy. Nevertheless Deuteronomy and its historical connection with Josiah's reform are important factors in the study of the Old Testament as a canon of sacred scripture. Its acceptance as the basis of Josiah's action shows a new form of canonical authority emerging in Israel.

The Form of Deuteronomy

One other feature has also achieved considerable prominence in recent study. This is the form which is given to the book of Deuteronomy. In the narrative account of Josiah's reform the book that was discovered, and which we have accepted as an earlier edition of Deuteronomy, is described as a 'covenant document'.[24]

[23] Cf. R. H. Pfeiffer, *ibid.*, p. 504a, 'The book of the law revealed to Moses was canonized in 621 B.C., but it marks the beginning, rather than the end, of a process'.

[24] II Kings 23.2. This is a preferable rendering of the Hebrew than 'book of the covenant'.

A considerable number of ancient oriental treaties, or covenant documents, ranging from the middle of the second millennium to the seventh century B.C., are now known. These come largely from the Hittite and Assyrian spheres and they reveal a treaty pattern of a remarkably uniform nature, although there are differences between the various examples which are by no means unimportant. These treaties have been closely studied, and their contents compared very carefully with the various accounts of covenants contained in the Old Testament.[25] In particular it has been suggested that the form of the Sinai covenant as a covenant of law, and the formulation of this law in the categorical I–Thou form, were both derived from this ancient oriental treaty form.[26] Exactly how, or when, Israel borrowed this form, however, remains obscure, and the closeness of the parallels between the oldest

[25] The literature on this subject is now very extensive, and the following studies may be mentioned as among the most accessible in English: G. E. Mendenhall, 'Covenant Forms in Israelite Tradition', *BA* 17, 1954, pp. 50-76; also the article 'Covenant' *IDB*, I, pp. 714 ff.; D. J. McCarthy, *Treaty and Covenant. A Study in Form in the Ancient Oriental Documents and in the Old Testament* (Analecta Biblica 21), Rome, 1963. A very valuable summary of the whole debate, with full bibliography, is given by McCarthy in *Der Gottesbund im Alten Testament* (SBS 13), Stuttgart, 1966. A shorter edition of this appeared in English as 'Covenant in the Old Testament: The Present State of Enquiry', *CBQ* 27, 1965, pp. 217-40. A convenient short account, with details of the most important oriental texts, is given by J. A. Thompson, *The Ancient Near Eastern Treaties and the Old Testament*, London, 1964.

[26] So especially G. E. Mendenhall, 'Ancient Oriental and Biblical Law', *BA* 17, 1954, pp. 26-46; W. Beyerlin, *Origins and History of the Oldest Sinaitic Traditions*, Oxford, 1965 pp. 50 ff.

accounts of the Sinai covenant and these treaties has been seriously questioned.[27] So also the claim that Israel derived its form of apodictic law from this treaty form has encountered firm opposition.[28]

Much sounder parallels can be adduced between the form of Deuteronomy and these political treaty documents,[29] although even here some insupportable conclusions have been put forward.[30] Nevertheless the fact of this formal similarity sets in a new light the arguments put forward by G. von Rad and G. E. Wright that the form of Deuteronomy has been deeply influenced by a cultic festival of covenant renewal.[31] While there is clearly a great deal in Deuteronomy which took its origin in the practices of Israel's worship, it is valuable to notice documentary parallels to it which show a marked similarity in form and style. That the authors of Deuteronomy were familiar with ancient treaty formulations is wholly probable. The eighth and seventh centuries in Israel were a period when the political dominance of Assyria was felt very

[27] Especially by D. J. McCarthy, *Treaty and Covenant*, pp. 159 ff.; *Der Gottesbund im A.T.*, pp. 29 ff.

[28] Particularly by E. Gerstenberger, 'Law and Covenant', *JBL* 84, 1965, pp. 38-51; and in *Wesen und Herkunft des 'apodiktischen Rechts'*, (WMANT 20), Neukirchen-Vluyn, 1965.

[29] Especially see D. J. McCarthy, *Treaty and Covenant*, pp. 109 ff., *Der Gottesbund im A.T.*, pp. 29 ff.

[30] Particularly by M. G. Kline, *The Treaty of the Great King. The Covenant Structure of Deuteronomy: Studies and Commentary*, Grand Rapids, 1963, who seeks to use such form-critical studies to prove a second millennium date for Deuteronomy.

[31] G. E. Wright, 'Deuteronomy', p. 326; G. von Rad, *Deuteronomy. A Commentary*, pp. 12, 23, 26.

powerfully, and Israel's kings were forced to submit to its imperial might. This undoubtedly involved the acceptance of a vassal relationship, expressed by submission to a treaty of the type we have been considering. No historical difficulty stands in the way of accepting that the authors of Deuteronomy were familiar with such conventions of diplomacy, which they could well have adapted to their own religious ends.[32]

This makes it possible to understand Deuteronomy as a covenant document, without necessarily supposing that it grew up as a written transcript of a cultic celebration of covenant renewal. At the same time it does not preclude that in its hortatory style, and in certain of its parts, the influence of the cult is present. Indeed it is very probable that the form of treaty documents reflects the form of covenant ceremonies. Thus the written document reflected the situation of its institution. As a result of these studies of the form of Deuteronomy we have a very much deepened insight into its character as a covenant document. It is now possible to see Deuteronomy within the context of covenant institutions of the Near East, both in their ritual and literary aspects.

The modern reader may be prompted to ask how relevant the book of Deuteronomy, with its questioning of established institutions and its desire to search out the very sources of spiritual life, is to our present-day situation. It cannot be too strongly urged that relevance is a quality that must be found rather than created. When we come to a biblical book our first

[32] Cf. D. J. McCarthy's remarks in a review of D. R. Hillers, *Treaty Curses and the Old Testament Prophets*, Rome, 1964, in *CBQ* 27, 1965, pp. 68 f.

task is to ask: Who were the authors? Why was it written? What were the problems of those for whom it was written? What was the purpose that the book was designed to serve? When we put these questions, and look at some of the answers that modern study can offer to us, we may very well find that we are learning about people who were much closer to ourselves than we at first supposed. We may well discover that their insights were not lacking in spiritual sensitivity, nor were their ambitions so very dissimilar from our own. We may learn to see in their work, and even in their mistakes as well as achievements, a valuable source of guidance for our own spiritual tasks.

2

THE COVENANT PEOPLE
OF GOD

DEUTERONOMY is composed in the form of an address to the people of Israel, and it soon becomes apparent that this Israel is regarded as a unity. This is all the more significant in view of the appearance of the book at a time when the nation had been deeply divided into two rival kingdoms for three centuries. In Deut. 1.1 the people are called 'all Israel', which is a very expressive title throughout the whole of the Deuteronomistic History. In Deuteronomy the people are sometimes addressed in the singular, and sometimes in the plural, providing a headache for the scholar who wishes to find the reason for the change, and to track down the various sources and revisions which have produced the present work. There is no reason to doubt, however, that even when Israel was addressed in the singular it was not normally individual members of the nation who were being singled out, but the nation as a whole. There is a quite extraordinary solidarity accorded to the nation which extends throughout all its members, and even binds together the succession of generations. The day on which Moses delivered his speech to Israel, before its entry into the promised land, passes almost imperceptibly over into the day when his words were read and reaffirmed to generations of Israelites long afterwards.[1] The interval of time which separated those who came out of Egypt from the people of Israel living in the land of Canaan is overcome by a sense of the fundamental unity which bound all Israel together. The words of Moses are intended for every citizen of this nation extending across its history as well as throughout the variety of its individual members. Deuteronomy nowhere exhorts Israel to unity, because it presupposes this unity as a fact, given by God when he bound Israel in covenant to himself.

A Holy People

We notice furthermore that Israel is not only a united body of people, but it also forms a nation with all those features which go to make up a national life. It lives upon a land which, Deuteronomy insists, has been given to it by God.[2] It may have a king to rule over it, like all the nations round about.[3] It may wage war against other nations,[4] and it may administer its own courts of law.[5] It even has regulations determining the conditions upon which people of certain other races may participate in the religious life of Israel.[6] In a great number of ways Deuteronomy pronounces its rulings and delivers its exhortations to an audience which it can define as a nation, and which formed one very small nation among a host of others in the world

[1] Cf. Deut. 4.4, 8, 20, 38 ff.; 5.1, 3, etc. We may compare the 'today' of Ps. 95.7.

[2] Deut. 4.38, 40; 6.18 f., 23, etc.   [3] Deut. 17.14 ff.

[4] Deut. 23.9 ff.   [5] Deut. 25.1 ff.   [6] Deut. 23.1 ff.

of the ancient Near East. In the political sense Israel
is regarded by Deuteronomy as possessed of full rights
of self government, with a legitimate national interest
to defend.

Yet for all its national and political status Israel is
not like any other nation, but is regarded as quite
distinct from them. The reason for this is very clearly
described:

For you are a people holy to the Lord your God; the
Lord your God has chosen you to be a people for his own
possession, out of all the peoples that are on the face of the
earth (Deut. 7.6. Cf. Deut. 4.20; 14.2; 26.18 f.).

The uniqueness of Israel is fully disclosed in the
brief phrase 'a people holy to the Lord your God'. What
makes the citizens of Israel different from the citizens
of any other country is the fact that they are in a sacred
relationship to Yahweh as their national God. This
holiness may conjure up to our modern minds a variety
of different, and perhaps conflicting, ideas. On the one
hand it may suggest a picture of people hag-ridden by
taboos, and conscience stricken about meaningless
infringements of divine commands. On the other it
may provide us with a mental image of men and
women who were striving every day for a better and a
nobler life. Neither picture in fact is a particularly
appropriate one, although it is certainly true that both
of them concern ideas of holiness which have developed out of the Old Testament assertions.

In the first place it is important to recognize that
the holiness of Israel of which Deuteronomy speaks is
an established fact, not a spiritual ambition. Israel is
holy by virtue of the specially tight bond which binds

it to God. As we shall see, this link was forged by God and not by the members of Israel, and this point is strongly insisted on in Deuteronomy. Israel cannot 'take time to be holy', because by its very existence it is holy. The particular laws which Deuteronomy outlines were given to Israel as an indication of the way in which, as a nation, it was to express this holiness. It was commanded to keep the law because it was a holy people, and not because it hoped to become one. This indicates to us a fundamental aspect of the idea of holiness in Deuteronomy. It is a term of relation, denoting the fact that Israel is in a special relationship to God which it cannot evade, because it has been brought about by historical circumstances. Israel's holiness is an act of God, not an act of man. All the various detailed regulations which appear in the laws of Deuteronomy are the outworking of this primary belief in the holiness of Israel, and they are intended to serve as guidelines to enable Israel to live up to its privileged position. They point out the way by which Israel can become, in practical expression, what it already is in theological affirmation. Admittedly Deuteronomy was not the first of Israel's documents to assert this fact of Israel's holiness, since such an assertion goes back to the earliest tradition of the covenant which God made on Mount Sinai (Ex. 19.5-6).[7] What was new in Deuter-

---

[7] This short section is studied in detail by H. Wildberger, *Jahwes Eigentumsvolk* (ATANT 37), Zürich, 1960, *passim*, who separates it from an original location on Sinai, and regards it as having taken its basic form at Gilgal. While certain doubts must remain as to how closely Ex. 19.5-6 records the original terms of the Sinai covenant, there is no doubt that this section is pre-Deuteronomic, and forms a basic foundation of the Deuteronomic theology.

onomy was the attempt to show in such detail what this holiness meant when applied to social, political and religious problems of everyday life. Israel's welfare as the people of God could not be left to the priests to care for, nor to the political rulers, but was to be brought to the level of everyone's concern and responsibility. The idea of holiness was carried into the world of everyday business and leisure, and made a guiding principle of conduct. The consequence of this was undoubtedly to give a stronger ethical colouring to the concept of holiness. Israel's status as a holy people was interpreted as a particular way of private and national life. Even such national responsibilities as military defence were controlled by very precise regulations derived from Israel's awareness of its relationship to God—in fact nowhere is the idea of holiness more evident than in the restrictions which it imposed on the conduct of an army in the field.[8]

The existence of Israel as a holy people is a basic presupposition of everything that Deuteronomy has to say, and has undoubtedly influenced the form of the book as an address to the nation. Our familiarity with such an idea may lead us at first to overlook its remarkable nature, and the surprising tensions which it inevitably produced. By accepting the fact of Israel's existence as a national state, with all that this implied in the way of political responsibility, Deuteronomy accepted that it had to legislate for everybody. The nation was regarded as a unity, and no exceptions were

[8] Deut. 20.1 ff.; 21.10 ff. For the nature and background of this concept of the holy war in Deuteronomy see G. von Rad, *Studies in Deuteronomy*, pp. 45 ff., and R. de Vaux, *Ancient Israel. Its Life and Institutions*, London, 1961, pp. 264 f.

envisaged to the demands which were made in consequence of the nation's holiness. No citizen was permitted to excuse himself from keeping the law, and certainly no freedom of religious choice was conceded. Israel as a whole had been committed by God to obey his will. This certainly did not mean that other religions could not exist—for other nations this is fully conceded[9]—but no other religion could exist for Israel. Deuteronomy would not tolerate that any citizen of Israel should have any other religion than that which had been established in the nation by God. Thus there was only to be one religion for the land and people of Israel, and any alien religious practice was to be ruthlessly dealt with.

The particular horror of the Deuteronomists was that vestiges of the beliefs and practices of the pre-Israelite inhabitants of Canaan should continue. These are made the object of the strictest prohibitions because of their offensive nature, and any participation in them is made a capital crime.[10] It is on this account that the pre-Israelite inhabitants are threatened with extermination. The apparent brutality of this ruling must be understood in the light of Deuteronomy's appearance long after the actual age of the conquest. These conquered peoples had long since ceased to exist as independent communities, and Deuteronomy was determined to prevent any continuance, or revival, of their religious practices. Even in the seventh century B.C., when Deuteronomy appeared, these ancient religious rites had not disappeared, and we must not suppose that Deuteronomy was really making a veiled

[9] Cf. especially Deut. 4.19.
[10] Deut. 6.14; 7.1 ff., 25 f.; 8.19 f.; 13.1 ff.

condemnation of imported Assyrian religious practices. Deuteronomy was not preaching a hatred of Gentile nations, but a hatred of false religious teachings and practices. It was not only concerned to educate Israel, but was intent also upon removing every source of error which could undermine that teaching.

The fact that Deuteronomy reckons with a state and a state religion inevitably left certain tensions in Israel, and raises questions in our minds. The kind of response which Deuteronomy demanded, and the measure of obedience which it required, could only have been given on an individual basis. Every citizen in the nation had to express his own personal responsibility to God by his conduct and his attitude. This is evident, not only in the details of legislation, but also in the repeated exhortations directed to the hearts and wills of individual hearers. In the personal response of each Israelite ultimately lay the response of Israel as a whole. We now recognize that it is impossible to expect an entire nation to react unanimously to any situation or appeal. Each person sees things differently, and responds differently to a given situation. Even the stirring pleas and warnings of the Deuteronomic preachers seem only to have provoked a mixed response. The parable of the Sower in the New Testament[11] expresses brilliantly both the nature of the gospel proclamation of the Kingdom of God, and also the whole enigma of Israel's history. From the days of its wilderness wandering some within Israel had learnt to grumble at the grace of God, and had scoffed at their own election. Only a part of the nation had remained faithful to God, giving rise to the conception of a

[11] Mark 4.3 ff. and par.

saving remnant. Deuteronomy, however, has no doctrine of a remnant, and ignores the possibility of such.[12] It is concerned with the nation as a whole, and is still hopeful that everyone can be persuaded to respond to the call of God. It is only after the failure of the Deuteronomic reform, and the political catastrophes that quickly followed, that we find a growing emphasis upon the idea of the remnant in Israel. Israel became a church of loyal individuals rather than a nation. Deuteronomy therefore stands out as a last great attempt to call Israel to national reform, including everyone in its appeal to repentance and renewal. The basic conviction that underlies this appeal is that Israel is a holy nation.

The Covenant of Horeb

The concept of Israel's holiness is related by Deuteronomy to the belief that a covenant exists between Yahweh and Israel made on Mount Horeb (Sinai), in which Moses acted as a mediator. This provides the point of union between God and his people, and the fact of its having been negotiated is a presupposition of all that Deuteronomy has to say, and has undoubtedly governed the presentation of the book as a historical discourse given by Moses. It is a 'covenant document', and no more apt description of Deuteronomy could be found.

[12] Cf. especially G. von Rad, *Das Gottesvolk im Deuteronomium* (BWANT III; 11), Stuttgart, 1929, pp. 17 f., 38 f. An embryonic doctrine of a remnant appears in Deut. 4.27-31, but this was not part of the original book, and must certainly be regarded as a later exilic, or even post-exilic, expansion.

Recent studies of the various covenants mentioned in the Old Testament have brought out several significant points. First we cannot treat the covenant purely as a 'concept' or an 'idea', as though it were a theological construction designed to explain the relationship of God to men. Covenants were essentially institutions, related to the social and political structures of a community, and vesting them with stability and a certain ideological content. Secondly there was no single unitary covenant, or covenant concept, in ancient Israel, but rather the recollection of a number of covenants which were not without historical relation to each other. In particular the Old Testament presents us with accounts of three major covenants which expressed a relationship between Yahweh and Israel. The first is the covenant between Yahweh and Abraham,[13] in which Abraham received a divine promise that his descendants would become a nation, and would take possession of the land of Canaan. The second is the covenant of Sinai, to which the law codes of the Decalogue and the Book of the Covenant were linked.[14] The third is the royal covenant between Yahweh and the house of David.[15]

Of these three Deuteronomy places all its emphasis

[13] Gen. 15 (J+); 17 (P). For this covenant see my study *Abraham and David. Genesis 15 and its Meaning for Israelite Tradition* (SBT, New Series 5), London, 1967.

[14] Ex. 19-34 (J, E & P). See especially W. Beyerlin, *The Origins and History of the Oldest Sinaitic Traditions*, Oxford, 1965, and M. L. Newman, *The People of the Covenant. A Study of Israel from Moses to the Monarchy*, London, 1965.

[15] II Sam. 7. For detailed references to literature see my *God and Temple. The Idea of the Divine Presence in Ancient Israel*. Oxford, 1965, pp. 55 ff.

upon the covenant of Horeb, the name by which it refers to the mountain otherwise known as Sinai. The book itself is presented as a document containing additional laws given by Moses after the making of the covenant on Mount Horeb.[16] The primary stipulations of this covenant are regarded as contained in the Ethical Decalogue (Deut. 5.6-21), and the code of Deuteronomy is presented as a later revelation given in the plains of Moab on the eve of the entry into the land. Deuteronomy is thus a document of the covenant of Horeb:

And Moses summoned all Israel, and said to them, 'Hear, O Israel, the statutes and the ordinances which I speak in your hearing this day, and you shall learn them and be careful to do them. The Lord our God made a covenant with us in Horeb. Not with our fathers did the Lord make this covenant, but with us, who are all of us here alive this day' (Deut. 5.1-2).

Here the Horeb covenant is presented as central to Israel's life, and its existence provides a sanction and authority for the laws which Deuteronomy gives. The insistence that Yahweh did not make this covenant with Israel's ancestors is put very strongly, and the language certainly goes beyond the normal demands requisite for a cultic ceremony of covenant renewal. Its purpose is to show that the covenant and the law by which Israel lived were given through Moses on Horeb, and the patriarchal covenant is presented as subordinate to this. Therefore, although Deuteronomy develops the traditions of both the patriarchal and the Sinaitic covenants, it relates them to each other in a

[16] Deut. 4.44 ff.

39

way which shows the greater significance attached to the latter. Yet the tradition of the covenant with Abraham is not ignored. On the contrary it is given a prominent position in the introductory discourses, and is regarded as a covenant made with all three major patriarchs.[17] The patriarchal and the Horeb covenants are related to each other in a scheme of promise and fulfilment. In the view of the Deuteronomists it was through the Horeb covenant that Yahweh's promise to the patriarchs was brought to fulfilment in Israel's becoming a nation and acquiring the land of Canaan. A considerable importance is attached, therefore, to the tradition of the Abrahamic covenant, but it is given a new meaning for Israel in relation to the covenant of Horeb. Consequently it does not represent an independent covenant tradition, but one which affirms the centrality of God's revelation through Moses.

This Deuteronomic covenant theology becomes even more interesting when we relate it to the fact that the earlier Jerusalem court tradition had closely connected the Abrahamic and the Davidic covenants to each other.[18] Deuteronomy makes no mention whatsoever of a separate dynastic covenant upon which Israel's monarchy rested. Admittedly the authors could not have referred explicitly to David without introducing an anachronism into their work, but they did introduce a law of the king:

When you come to the land which the Lord your God gives you, and you possess it and dwell in it, and then say, 'I will set a king over me, like all the nations that are

[17] Deut. 1.8, 11; 4.31; 6.10; 7.12; 8.18; 9.5, 27; 11.9
[18] Cf. G. E. Mendenhall, 'Covenant Forms in Israelite Tradition', pp. 72 ff., and my *Abraham and David*, pp. 54 ff.

round about me'; you may indeed set as king over you him
whom the Lord your God will choose. One from among
your brethren you shall set as king over you; you may not
put a foreigner over you, who is not your brother. Only
he must not multiply horses for himself, or cause the
people to return to Egypt in order to multiply horses,
since the Lord has said to you, 'You shall never return
that way again.' And he shall not multiply wives for himself, lest his heart turn away; nor shall he greatly multiply
for himself silver and gold (Deut. 17.14-17).

This law cannot simply be a reflection of a distinctive attitude to the kingship which had grown up in
the Northern Kingdom after the disruption of the
Davidic–Solomonic empire, although its rejection of
the conduct of Solomon is very explicit. It has a polemical intention, and it is most probable that this is to
be seen in the insistence that the future king is to be 'one
from among your brethren'. This must be a rejection
of the view that the Israelite king was uniquely God's
'son', which was undoubtedly the view of the monarchy
which was current in the Jerusalem-Davidic tradition.[19] It is hard for us to avoid the conclusion that the
Deuteronomists were deliberately introducing a law
of the kingship which repudiated one of the foundation stones of the religio-political structure of the state
of Judah. They must have framed, therefore, their law
with the Jerusalem royal tradition in mind. Consequently, their failure to make any reference to the
covenant with Yahweh on which this royal Davidic
ideology was based can have been no accident. They

[19] Cf. especially Pss. 2.7; 89.26; II Sam. 7.14 and see G.
Cooke, 'The Israelite King as Son of God', *ZAW* 73, 1961, pp.
202-25.

were deliberately rejecting the idea that Israel's monarchy was based on a separate covenant with a royal dynasty through which the divine authority over the nation was expressed. For them this belief was no longer an acceptable interpretation of the relationship between Yahweh and Israel.

How are we to explain this rejection of the tradition of the Davidic covenant by the Deuteronomists in favour of focusing all Israel's life on the Mosaic revelation at Horeb and in the plains of Moab? Certainly part of the explanation must lie in the particular traditions and background which the Deuteronomists had inherited. Thus their interpretation of the kingship has provided a strong support for the view that they derived from the Northern Kingdom, where we know that the tradition of a covenant between Yahweh and the house of David was unacceptable. Yet this geographical and political background may not be the whole explanation of this distinctive Deuteronomic viewpoint. They were not merely echoing an old tradition which interpreted the monarchy in a very different way from the court circle of Jerusalem, but were directly concerned to oppose the religious basis on which the Jerusalem tradition rested. Why was this?

The explanation of the Deuteronomic law must surely lie in its opposition to a fundamental feature of the content of the Davidic covenant tradition. Not only did this give an exalted religious status to the king, but it asserted that this covenant was permanent and unconditional in its character. It is revealed to us in Israelite tradition as a covenant that was to endure 'for ever'.[20] No stipulations were attached to it as con-

[20] II Sam. 7.16; 23.5; I Kings 2.45; Pss. 89.4, 29, 36, 37; 110.4.

ditions for its continued existence, although there was an obligation on the part of David's descendants to be loyal and obedient to Yahweh. Even in this, however, the tradition explicitly stated that disobedience would not result in the annulling of the covenant, but only in the chastening of the king concerned.[21] Thus the Davidic covenant had been believed to provide a divine assurance that Israel's relationship to God was permanently secured through the Davidic monarch who sat upon its throne. It is this notion that a permanent and unconditional bond existed between Yahweh and Israel through the Davidic covenant that is rejected by the Deuteronomists. For them the relationship to Yahweh, which is the foundation of the nation's life, was seen to be established in the covenant of Horeb with its law. There was no other covenant which obviated this, or which lessened the stringency of the demand for obedience to the law's commands.

Thus the distinctive character of the Deuteronomic teaching regarding the covenant basis of Israel lies in its unifying character, in which the various covenant traditions which were current in Israel were brought into harmony. At the same time there is a strong insistence that the covenant declares to Israel a law, and upon Israel's attitude to this law hinges the fate of the nation. This note of urgency, which sounds through-

---

[21] II Sam. 7.14-15; Ps. 89.30-7. In Ps. 132.12 obedience does seem to be a condition of the covenant, but this may simply be an apparent exception arising from the hymnic form. The view of the Deuteronomistic historian, who was undoubtedly following the attitude of the Deuteronomists who framed the law of the kingship is noticeably different. See I Kings 3.14; 8.25; 11.11 ff., where obedience to the Mosaic law becomes a condition of Yahweh's acceptance of the king.

out the book, is not only the echo of a religious crisis, but also of a historical one. Israel in the seventh century B.C. was facing a situation in which its very existence might be brought to an end, as had already happened to a large part of the nation in the Northern Kingdom.

The covenant to which Deuteronomy unerringly points is the covenant of Horeb-Sinai, and the prescriptions of the Deuteronomic *tōrāh* are regarded as the Mosaic instruction given in the plains of Moab prior to the entry into Canaan. It is a supplement to the basic covenant law of the Decalogue.[22] Thus Deuteronomy is essentially a document of the Horeb covenant. In Deut. 29, however, there is reference to a covenant made in the land of Moab, besides that made at Horeb, and this is regarded as the covenant ceremony in which Deuteronomy was delivered to the nation. This covenant in the land of Moab is referred to only in Deuteronomy, and far from pointing to an ancient institution, it appears as a relatively late tradition arising out of earlier Deuteronomic material. Almost all commentators are agreed in asserting that Deut. 29-30 formed no part of the original Deuteronomy, and are a subsequent addition to the book.[23] The covenant to which Deuteronomy points is the Horeb covenant itself, and

[22] Deut. 5.1 ff.

[23] G. E. Wright, 'Deuteronomy', pp. 502 f. G. von Rad, *Deuteronomy. A Commentary*, pp. 178 f. For a detailed study of this Moab covenant see especially N. Lohfink, 'Der Bundesschluss im Land Moab. Redaktionsgeschichtliches zu Dt. 28, 69-32, 47', *BZ* 6, 1962, pp. 32-56. Both Wright and Lohfink see a cultic ceremony underlying the account in Deut. 29, and Lohfink particularly connects this with the form of vassal treaties.

the book is written as an explication of the demands which this enjoined upon Israel. Israel's status as a holy people was conferred upon it by the bond which God established at Horeb, and which set before the nation the laws which defined how this holiness was to be expressed.

The Divine Election

In Deuteronomy the divine action which instituted the covenant is described for the first time as an act of election.[24] This both emphasizes the fact of divine grace which established Israel's covenant relationship to God, and also relates this to the existence of other nations. Thus Israel's privileged position before God is made the subject of careful reflection, and the consequences of this for other nations are more consciously brought to the fore. The concepts of holiness and covenant relationship are brought to focus in a doctrine of divine election in which Israel's very existence as a nation is made the subject of theological interpretation:

For you are a people holy to the Lord your God, and the Lord has chosen you to be a people for his own possession, out of all the peoples that are on the face of the earth (Deut. 14.2).

Here we are first presented explicitly with the claim that Israel is a chosen nation, although it is undoubtedly true that the earlier belief in a covenant between Israel and God went a considerable way towards imply-

[24] Deut. 7.6 ff.; 14.2. On this concept see especially G. E. Mendenhall, 'Election', *IDB*, II, pp. 79 ff.

ing this. Before this time, however, the idea of election was explicitly current in Israel in relation to the Davidic kingship of Jerusalem, and the divine dwelling upon Mount Zion.[25] These were certainly not unrelated to the broader concept that Israel as a whole was chosen by God. Yahweh's elect king and his elect sanctuary were signs of his relationship to Israel, and witnessed to his authority over the whole nation. They were thus related to the belief in the Davidic covenant with its promises, and like this were said to be 'for ever'. In this Jerusalem court tradition the election of Israel was regarded as mediated by, and dependent upon, the election of the Davidic monarchy and the temple which had been founded by this monarchy.

Deuteronomy is familiar with, and affirms, belief both in the divine election of Israel's kings, and of Yahweh's sanctuary.[26] What was new with this book, therefore, was not the coining of the term 'election', but its explicit application to cover the whole Israelite nation. Not simply the king, nor the nation's shrine, but the whole nation was regarded as the object of God's special choice.

It is noteworthy therefore that Deuteronomy connects this act of divine election with the Horeb covenant, and not with the Davidic. Once again there is a deliberate passing over of the Davidic covenant in favour of that of Horeb. Neither the Davidic dynasty

[25] The election of Mount Zion is expressed in I Kings 8.12-13; Pss. 78.69; 132.14. The election of David and his sons is referred to in the terms of the Davidic covenant. Both acts of divine choice were said to be 'for ever'.
[26] Of God's appointed sanctuary: Deut. 12.5, 11, 14; 16.11, 16; of Israel's king: Deut. 17.15.

46

nor the Jerusalem temple are regarded as the outward guarantees of Israel's elect status, although both of them are conceded a legitimate place in the nation's religious life. Election is related to the Horeb covenant with its tablets of law, and to the covenant document of Deuteronomy. The divine word, rather than the sacred king and temple, is the witness to Israel that it is the chosen people of God.

This complete recasting of the concept of election by the Deuteronomists cannot be explained simply as an opposition on their part to the monarchy as such. The place of the king is fully recognized, although within limits. It was the particular content and character of the earlier Israelite doctrine of election which was unacceptable to these men. Influenced no doubt by the traditions of the Northern Kingdom, and by their knowledge of its downfall, the Deuteronomists presented Israel's election in relation to the Horeb covenant and its law. The Israelite kingship, and the sanctuary which it had founded, were consequences, but not guarantees, of this election.

This introduced a new element into the Deuteronomic understanding of Israel's election, since the law became the witness to Israel of its privileged status before God. It was not, however, regarded as a condition of Israel's election, which is forcefully described as a free act of divine grace:

It was not because you were more in number than any other people that the Lord set his love upon you and chose you, for you were the fewest of all peoples; but it is because the Lord loves you, and is keeping the oath which he swore to your fathers, that the Lord has brought you out with a mighty hand, and redeemed you from the house of bondage, from the hand of Pharaoh king of Egypt (Deut. 7.7-8).

Here the nation's election is traced to the two basic facts of God's love for Israel and his covenant with its ancestors. In this way the patriarchal covenant is introduced by the Deuteronomists in relation to the covenant of Horeb, and is seen as declaring the election which the latter brought to realization.

This use of the tradition of the covenant with the patriarchs, which in the earlier history is centred on Abraham, relates the age of the patriarchs to that of Moses in a scheme of promise and fulfilment. The covenant with Abraham is interpreted by Deuteronomy as a covenant of election, and the events of the exodus, the making of the covenant on Mount Horeb, and the conquest of the land of Canaan, are all seen as fulfilling this declared intention of God. While Israel did not actually become the people of God until the institution of the covenant on Mount Horeb, the fact of the divine election which brought this about had earlier been foretold to Abraham, Isaac and Jacob. It is significant, therefore, that when Moses faced the possibility of Israel's destruction by God in the wilderness for its obstinacy, he appealed in his prayer to the knowledge of the patriarchal covenant:

Remember thy servants, Abraham, Isaac and Jacob; do not regard the stubbornness of this people, or their wickedness, their sin (Deut. 9.27).

Even though Israel had sinned against the laws of the covenant of Horeb, yet still the mystery of God's electing love remained, and Moses appealed to the memory of the patriarchs as the historical figures through whom this divine love had been made known. We can see in this brief reference that Deuteronomy, in its presentation of this intercessory prayer of Moses, was very conscious of the challenge presented by human sin to the will and purpose of God for his people. Deuteronomy asserted as clearly as possible that God is gracious without being indulgent, and righteous without ceasing to be merciful. Election is not a human achievement, but a gift of God, and it was this to which the patriarchal covenant testified. Thus, in the Deuteronomic view, the patriarchal and the Horeb covenants were not two separate institutions, but were seen to be parts of the one great mystery of God's choice of Israel to be his holy people. Grace and law were as inseparable as promise and fulfilment. Each pointed in its own way to the same central reality of a divine purpose involving the history and destiny of Israel.

3

THE GIFTS OF GOD

WE have seen in the preceding chapter the very strong emphasis which is placed by Deuteronomy upon the divine grace which brought Israel into existence, and which bound it to God by a covenant. Israel was a people under a great debt to God. This stress on the goodness of God runs through the whole book, colouring its presentation of history and motivating the laws which it establishes. God, in his love, has given to his people innumerable gifts so that the primary motive of their obedience to him should be gratitude for what he has given.

The Land

First among these gifts is the land of Canaan, and the fact of this gift is a major theme of the hortatory speeches.[1] We have noted already that there was a close link between this promise of the land and the patriarchal covenant. It therefore becomes integral to the interpretation of Israel's election. For Israel to be a nation meant that it enjoyed full political control over

[1] Deut. 4.40; 5.16; 7.13; 11.9, 21; 21.1, 23; 25.15; 26.10, 15; 28.11, 63; 30.18, 20; 31.13, 20; 32.47.

the territory which had once belonged to the peoples of Canaan. People and land belonged together, since the ownership of the land was the badge of their nationhood. Yet there was no mystical bond uniting Israel with the soil which it tilled, but only a truly religious one derived from the knowledge that Israel had taken possession of this land in the course of a divinely controlled history. Thus Israel's right to its land was through and through interpreted theologically:

Do not say in your heart, after the Lord your God has thrust them out before you, 'It is because of my righteousness that the Lord has brought me in to possess the land'; whereas it is because of the wickedness of these nations that the Lord is driving them out before you. Not because of your righteousness or the uprightness of your heart are you going in to possess their land; but because of the wickedness of these nations the Lord your God is driving them out from before you, and that he may confirm the word which the Lord swore to your fathers, to Abraham, to Isaac, and to Jacob (Deut. 9.4-5).

Any claim that Israel had a natural right to this land was swept aside by the assertion that Israel had come into possession of it on account of the gross misbehaviour of the previous inhabitants. Thus the land was conceived as a sacred trust, granted to Israel on condition that it remained faithful to the laws of the God who had given it. While the sins of the Canaanites had brought about their expulsion from the land, it was not for any corresponding virtue that Israel had been given possession of it. Rather this was because God had willed it so in fulfilment of his promise to the patriarchs.

This divine gift of the land provides a major theme of the Deuteronomic teaching, and its repeated assertion is a controlling motive for the regulations governing social and religious behaviour:

For the Lord your God is bringing you into a good land, a land of brooks of water, of fountains and springs, flowing forth in valleys and hills, a land of wheat and barley, of vines and fig trees and pomegranates, a land of olive trees and honey, a land in which you will eat bread without scarcity, in which you will lack nothing, a land whose stones are iron, and out of whose hills you can dig copper. And you shall eat and be full, and you shall bless the Lord your God for the good land he has given you (Deut. 8.7-10).

Here we are shown that the land was regarded as the primary source of all Israel's economic wealth, for out of it came all those raw materials and produce which were to make it prosperous. The land was the fundamental wealth which provided the basis for the prosperity of individual families and the nation as a whole. Deuteronomy thus teaches a 'holy materialism' which recognized the right of Israel to material advancement and to the enjoyment of the fruits of the land, but which also insisted that this right belonged to the spiritual order of things, and not to any natural law:

Beware lest you say in your heart, 'My power and the might of my hand have gotten me this wealth. You shall remember the Lord your God, for it is he who gives you power to get wealth; that he may confirm his covenant which he swore to your fathers, as at this day' (Deut. 8.17-18).

The assertion that Israel's possession of the land of Canaan is a divinely given gift brings every aspect of material and economic life into the sphere of religion. There is in fact, in the Deuteronomic teaching, no divorce between the sacred and the secular, and no division between the material and spiritual realms, for everyday life is stamped with the seal of God's holiness, and material possessions are related to Israel's covenant with God.

The religious significance of Israel's enjoyment of its land becomes an important motive for several of the laws which the code of Deuteronomy lays down. Because land is the basic form of wealth it must be protected against misuse and exploitation, and its benefits must be shared with those who are unfortunate enough to have no private allotment. Thus the tithes of every third year are to be set aside for the support of Levites, orphans, widows and foreign residents who do not have land holdings of their own.[2] Even more striking is the way in which Deuteronomy forbids certain actions because they are considered to 'defile' the land, or to 'bring guilt' upon it.[3] Because possession of the land is invested with a religious significance the moral behaviour of those who live upon it is regarded as affecting the land itself.

In the religions of Israel's neighbours, and also in that of the Canaanite peoples who had once lived on Israel's land, a very close link was believed to exist between the land and the deities who were worshipped on it. The gods were the owners of the land, and its use

[2] Deut. 14.28-9; cf. Deut. 24.19-22.
[3] Deut. 21.23, where it is laid down that a criminal whose corpse is hanged after execution is to be buried the same day; for a hanged man is accursed by God; 'you shall not defile your land which the Lord your God gives you for an inheritance'.

was only permitted to men provided they gave proper tribute to these divine landlords in the form of tithes and offerings. The authors of Deuteronomy were certainly familiar with such ancient religious beliefs, but they consciously avoided them, and rejected any notion that the land was itself filled with divine power. Their interpretation of the religious significance of the land is made distinctive by its concern for history. Israel had not always possessed this land, but had acquired it through a campaign of conquest which God himself had led.[4] There was, therefore, no magical or mythological association between the land of Canaan and the people of Israel. Israel came to possess it through certain historical events. Similarly there was no direct connection between the land and God, as though the land were in itself divine or were filled with divine power. Everything which gave legal and religious significance to the land was governed by a sense of history, and by an awareness of the events which had brought both land and people together.

This sense of history attaching to the land becomes the subject of a remarkable religious confession intended to be used by worshippers when they brought the gifts of the firstfruits of their harvest to God as an acknowledgment of their debt to God for the gift of the land:

And you shall go to the priest who is in office at that time, and say to him, 'I declare this day to the Lord your God that I have come into the land which the Lord swore to our fathers to give us' (Deut. 26.3).

The priest then accepts the basket of fruit from the

[4] Cf. Deut. 7.1-2; 9.1-3.

worshipper, who is given the following confession to make:

A wandering Aramean was my father; and he went down into Egypt and sojourned there, few in number; and there he became a nation; great, mighty, and populous. And the Egyptians treated us harshly, and afflicted us, and laid upon us hard bondage. Then we cried to the Lord the God of our fathers, and the Lord heard our voice, and saw our affliction, our toil, and our oppression; and the Lord brought us out of Egypt with a mighty hand and an outstretched arm, with great terror, with signs and wonders; and he brought us into this place and gave us this land, a land flowing with milk and honey. And behold, now I bring the first of the fruit of the ground, which thou, O Lord, hast given me (Deut. 26.5b-10a).

This confession, which summarizes the main events of Israel's origins, is directed towards establishing the primary fact that Israel's land is a God-given gift, and everything that is grown upon it is a product of the providential history which brought Israel into possession of it.

In recent years the view of G. von Rad has been widely accepted. He holds that Deut. 26.5b-9 is a primitive creed, deriving from a period long before Deuteronomy, which described the sacred history in which Israel recognized the saving activity of its God.[5] On the basis of this view very far-reaching conclusions have been drawn regarding the growth of the Pentateuch and the Israelite conception of divine revelation.

[5] G. von Rad, 'The Form-Critical Problem of the Hexateuch', *The Problem of the Hexateuch and Other Essays*, Edinburgh, 1966, pp. 3 ff.

Yet it is by no means an established fact that Deut. 26.5b-9 is a primitive Israelite creed which is much older than Deuteronomy. Both the age and the character of this confession must be closely examined. Although von Rad was not the first to argue for its antiquity,[6] it appears much more probable that it is a Deuteronomic composition based upon the traditional history of Israel's origins. Instead of antedating the earliest Pentateuchal history it presupposes it.[7] It, therefore, cannot be used in support of the argument that the worship of early Israel made use of such short historical summaries as confessions of faith.

Furthermore it must be insisted upon that Deut. 26.5b-9 cannot be separated from v. 10 which forms the climax of the whole confession.[8] The purpose of the confession is not to provide a creed, declaring the revelation of God in history, but to show Israel how it came to be in possession of its land. This certainly presupposes that the history which brought this about has a revelatory significance, but it is not the events themselves, in isolation from their consequence, which possess this character. The purpose of the confession is to affirm that all that the Israelite farmer brings to God derives ultimately from God's prior gift of the land to him. Thus the history that is recalled finds its

[6] Cf. A. C. Welch, *The Code of Deuteronomy*, pp. 24 ff.

[7] Cf. C. H. W. Brekelmans, 'Het "historische Credo" van Israël', *Tijdschrift voor Theologie* 3, 1963, pp. 2 ff., 11. Th. C. Vriezen, *De godsdienst van Israel*, Zeist, 1963, pp. 134, 251. L. Rost, 'Das kleine geschichtliche Credo', *Das kleine Credo und andere Studien*, Heidelberg, 1965, pp. 11 ff. argues that these verses are an expansion of the original edition of Deuteronomy.

[8] C. H. W. Brekelmans, *op. cit.*, p. 8.

revelatory significance through the recognition that Israel's land is a gift of God.[9]

Through this significance attached to the land all of Israel's material wealth is given a religious meaning as God's gift, and all the produce of the land is regarded as derived ultimately from him. This is not simply because God controls the processes of nature, although this is fully accepted, but because Israel obtained control of its land through the gracious action of God. The realms of nature and of history are not regarded as separate compartments of life, but as united through their mutual control by God. His role as Creator is not distinct from his role as Lord of history, for both creation and history alike are expressions of his one will. Israel, therefore, could express its thanks to God for the benefits of the material order by recalling the historical events which had provided it with the opportunity of enjoying them.

Because the God who gave the land is the God of the covenant with its laws, there is a relationship between the land and the moral demands of God. It is not surprising, therefore, that the threat of losing possession of the land and its fruits is the fundamental punishment that is envisaged should Israel disobey God.[10] Possession of the land is the sign of Israel's

[9] Similarly with regard to the 'credo' which von Rad believes to find in Deut. 6.20-24. This section is thoroughly Deuteronomic in its phraseology, and cannot be older than the rest of the book. Cf. C. H. W. Brekelmans, *op. cit.*, pp. 4 ff., and N. Lohfink, *Das Hauptgebot. Eine Untersuchung literarischer Einleitungsfragen zu Dtn.* 5-11, Rome, 1963, pp. 159 ff. In this section, however, the history points to the giving of the law instead of the land.

[10] Deut. 4.25-26; cf. Deut. 8.19-20; 28.21, 24, 33, 36, 42, 51, 64 ff.

nationhood, and the continuing evidence of the goodness of God. A breach of the covenant is naturally seen
to have its consequence in expulsion from the land,
which is God's special gift.

The Law

The second of Yahweh's major gifts to Israel was
seen by the Deuteronomists to be the revelation of
the divine will in the sacred law. This was contained
in the tablets of the covenant and in the book of
Deuteronomy which supplemented them. We have
already pointed out that Deuteronomy describes this
law as *tōrāh*, and regards it as the substance of a continuing religious instruction of Israel. None the less it
never loses its character as law, as is shown by its
being defined as 'testimonies, statutes and ordinances'.
It presented the stipulations of Yahweh's covenant
made on Mount Horeb, and covered a wide range of
subjects, including the administration of justice, the
organization of worship, and even the composition of
Israel's army and its methods of waging war. Thus it
far exceeded the scope of law in the technical and
juridical sense, even in the 'legal' connotation given
to it by Deuteronomy.

Deuteronomy particularly emphasizes that the purpose of the law was not to bind Israel to a set of
arbitrary restrictions, but to guide it towards the
fullest enjoyment of life. Repeatedly it is stressed that
the law is given 'that it may go well with you', and
'that you may prolong your days in the land which the
Lord your God gives you'.[11] This must be interpreted

[11] Deut. 4.40; 5.33; 6.2, 18, 24; 11.9; 12.28; 13.17, 18.

not simply in the sense that God would reward the good behaviour of his people, but that the laws themselves were designed to increase the health and prosperity of men:

The Lord commanded us to do all these statutes, to fear the Lord our God, for our good always, that he might preserve us alive as at this day (Deut. 6.24).

Nowhere in the Old Testament is the grace of the law more emphatically declared than here. It is God's gift, showing how men can enjoy to the full the benefits of life and possessions which are also divinely given. The character of the divine *tōrāh* presented by Deuteronomy is therefore a gracious one.[12] Its purpose is to reveal to men the nature and reality of Yahweh's grace, and to show the quality of life which this demands:

You shall be careful to do therefore as the Lord your God has commanded you; you shall not turn aside to the right hand or to the left. You shall walk in all the way which the Lord your God has commanded you, that you may live, and that it may go well with you, and that you may live long in the land which you shall possess (Deut. 5.32-3).

The law, therefore, is in no sense presented as a burden upon Israel, but as a God-given source of guidance which was intended to enable Israel to enjoy its land and to prosper upon it. It is not a counterpart to divine grace, but a very important expression of it. Its purpose is not to reveal God's anger,

[12] Cf. G. von Rad, *Old Testament Theology*, I, Edinburgh and London, 1967, pp. 229 f., II, p. 395.

but his mercy, and only when the law is rejected or ignored does God's wrath become evident. Thus there is a very positive and saving function accorded to the law which Deuteronomy presents. Its fulfilment is not regarded as a serious problem, but as a simple question whether Israel will accept or refuse its obligation to obedience.

It is because the law has this saving and life-giving role to play in Israel's life that it is made the subject of such a determined effort of instruction. The head of every household was made responsible for teaching these laws to his children, and for ensuring that he himself did not forget them.[13] Behind this zeal for an understanding of the law by every Israelite citizen there lies the belief that it is a gift of God's love, and reveals this love to the nation.

Since the Deuteronomists placed such emphasis upon the responsibility of private individuals in Israel for furthering the religious education of the nation, it comes as no surprise that they also entrusted to the king, as the first citizen, the task of bringing to the nation the divine law:

When he sits on the throne of his kingdom, he shall write for himself in a book a copy of this law, from that which is in charge of the Levitical priests; and it shall be with him, and he shall read in it all the days of his life, that he may learn to fear the Lord his God, by keeping all the words of this law and these statutes, and doing them; that his heart may not be lifted up above his brethren, and that he may not turn aside from the commandment, either to the right hand or to the left; so that he may continue

---

[13] See above, pp. 13 f.

long in his kingdom, he and his children, in Israel (Deut. 17.18-20).[14]

This placing of the king in submission to the law of Moses is a further significant aspect of the Deuteronomic covenant theology. The earlier Jerusalem court tradition, with its belief in Yahweh's covenant with the Davidic dynasty, had regarded the king himself as a source of *tōrāh*.[15]

In its interpretation of the divine law as a saving gift, Deuteronomy is very far from legalism. Yet we cannot exonerate the book entirely from contributing to the legalism of later Judaism. Deuteronomy sets the divine law in the forefront of the covenant, and presents a certain 'legalizing' of the concept of *tōrāh* by equating it with the stipulations of the covenant. Because Israel's election and its covenant status were not in doubt, the law was a consequence, and not a condition, of this election. However, in making this law the primary sign of Israel's election, Deuteronomy makes an advance over earlier Israelite tradition. When that election was later placed in doubt through the political downfall of Judah and the end of the Davidic monarchy, it was natural that reassurance should be sought through the observance of the law. Although Deuteronomy itself, therefore, is not a legalistic book, it did create a regard for the law, in which legalism was a latent possibility.

[14] G. von Rad, *Deuteronomy. A Commentary*, p. 119, regards Deut. 17.18-20 as a later addition to the original law of the kingship. Cf. also G. E. Wright, 'Deuteronomy', p. 422.

[15] Cf. G. Östborn, *Tōrā in the Old Testament. A Semantic Study*, pp. 54 ff. For the outworking of such a view see I Kings 3.5 ff; Isa. 9.7; 11.2 ff.; Ps. 101.

This is further confirmed when we consider that Deuteronomy avoids the assertion that Yahweh has made his covenant with Israel 'for ever'.[16] It has no unconditional guarantees, but is morally conditioned by the stipulations which God has attached to it. The law is thereby set between God and Israel as a mediating instrument. Later disciples of the original authors of Deuteronomy seem to have felt the intolerable nature of this tension, and to have looked for a more positive assurance of God's destiny for Israel. This undoubtedly took place during the exile, and has left its mark on the later introductory sections of Deuteronomy.[17] The original Deuteronomy, however, regarded the law as facing Israel with a decision of life or death.[18]

The Prophets

As the land which Israel inhabited, and the law which it was to obey, had been given by God, so also the religious institutions and ministers of the nation were regarded as his gift. Of these a special interest attaches to Deuteronomy's concern for the prophets, since it is the only law code of the Old Testament to legislate for them. This it does in two passages. In the first of these[19] it firmly lays down that if any prophet incites an Israelite to worship any other God than Yahweh he is false, and must be put to death. Thus

[16] This phrase is used in connection with Israel's possession of its land in Deut. 4.40, where it is certainly a post-exilic addition. In 12.28 the promise is conditioned.

[17] Deut. 4.27-40.

[18] Deut. 11.26 ff.; 28.1 ff.; 30.15.   [19] Deut. 13.1-5.

Deuteronomy recognizes the presence of non-Yahwistic prophets in Israel's life, and demands their removal. This is carried still further in Deut. 18.20-22, where the more subtle difficulty is considered of prophets who prophesy in Yahweh's name, but who may, nevertheless, be false. Here the more general criterion is laid down:

When a prophet speaks in the name of the Lord, if the word does not come to pass or come true, that is a word which the Lord has not spoken; the prophet has spoken it presumptuously, you need not be afraid of him (Deut. 18.22).

There is a certain inconclusiveness in this injunction, since it can only have been of limited value in unmasking false prophets. None the less it reveals the underlying feeling of unease which was present to the Deuteronomists in their regard for prophecy. While firmly accepting the role of prophets in Israel's life, they were aware too that there had been false prophets, who had been the cause of misleading the nation and bringing harm upon it. They may have had in mind particularly those prophets who had assured Israel of its well-being in times of crisis, instead of alerting the nation to a sense of danger. The Northern Kingdom had fallen in ruins, and it appears that even to the end there had been prophets who had given false assurances to the people.[20] So also in Judah there had been prophets who cried 'Peace', when they should have warned the nation of coming disaster.[21]

Yet the voice of prophecy had not been wholly dis-

[20] Cf. Hos. 4.5.   [21] Cf. Micah 3.5 ff.

appointing, and in such figures as Amos, Hosea, Isaiah and Micah the sternest warnings had been set before Israel and Judah. Micah in particular warned Jerusalem that even the temple would not suffice to save it[22]—a declaration which must have found an echoing conviction in the hearts of the Deuteronomists. How then should prophecy be regarded? The most interesting assertion is made in Deut. 18.18; where God says to Moses:

I will raise up for them a prophet like you from among their brethren; and I will put my words in his mouth, and he shall speak to them all that I command him (Deut. 18.18).

Although later Judaism interpreted this in terms of a coming eschatological prophet,[23] this was most probably not its original intention. It referred to a prophet, or more probably a succession of prophets, who would continue the mediating office of Moses in Israel.[24] We must not construe this Mosaic 'office' too rigidly, or link it with any one particular institution in Israel. It connects the work of the prophets in mediating the divine will to Israel with the work of Moses. Thus the Deuteronomists are in line with Hosea in regarding Moses as a prophet.[25] This regard for Moses as a prophet has been thought to show an exceptional regard for prophecy, suggesting that the authors of

[22] Micah 3.9 ff.

[23] Cf. H. M. Teeple, *The Mosaic Eschatological Prophet* (Journal of Biblical Literature Monograph Series 10), Philadelphia, 1957.

[24] Cf. especially H. J. Kraus, *Worship in Israel. A Cultic History of the Old Testament*, Oxford, 1966, pp. 106 ff.

[25] Hos. 12.13.

Deuteronomy were themselves prophets. We have accepted, however, that this was not the case, and that they were Levitical priests. It is noteworthy, therefore, that Deuteronomy links prophecy with Moses in a way that must have been relatively new in Israel. The explanation of this may be in the intention that lies behind Deut. 18.15-20. This seeks to show, not only that Moses was a prophet, but that the prophets were not above Moses. The prophets maintained a continuing source of divine *tōrāh* for Israel, but this did not render the Mosaic *tōrāh* unnecessary. On the contrary the prophets presumed it, and confirmed its authority. Thus, in the view of the Deuteronomists, the prophets were given by God to confirm the truth and authority of the Mosaic revelation. This in fact is exactly what did occur in Josiah's reform when Huldah, the prophetess, affirmed the authenticity of the law book that had been discovered.[26] By relating the prophets to Moses the Deuteronomists showed that prophecy did not point away from the Mosaic law, but to it. Prophecy, too, therefore, was a gift of God, as was the law, and the two were to provide allied means whereby Israel was to know the will of God.

The Levites

The other religious ministry of Israel is provided by the Levites, who are mentioned frequently in Deuteronomy,[27] usually as 'the Levitical priests'. It appears that Deuteronomy assigns to all Levites

[26] II Kings 22.14 ff.
[27] Deut. 12.12, 18, 19; 14.27, 29; 16.11, 14; 17.9, 18; 18.1, 6, 7; 24.8; 26.11, 12, 13; 27.9, 14; 31.9, 25.

priestly functions, as becomes clear from Deut. 18.1:
'The Levitical priests, that is, all the tribe of Levi.'[28]
A. H. J. Gunneweg has argued that the origin of the
Levites is to be traced to a kind of religious order who
were especially dedicated to the service of Yahweh in
the old tribal amphictyony.[29] This is an interesting
suggestion, but one which lacks the support of any
really unequivocal evidence in the Old Testament.
The organization of the old amphictyony is far from
clear, and firm conclusions as to its religious structure
are seldom warranted. Even from the period of the
Judges the Old Testament traditions witness to the
fact that Israelites preferred to have a Levite as a
priest,[30] and Moses himself must have been a Levite.[31]
Not all priests were Levites, however.

Deuteronomy now urged that only Levites could be
priests, and that all Levites had the right to perform
priestly duties. At the same time there is in Deut.
18.6-7 an awareness that some Levites lived in the

[28] G. E. Wright, 'The Levites in Deuteronomy', *VT* 4, 1954,
pp. 325-30, has argued that this should be translated 'the priests,
the Levites, *and* all the tribe of Levi', in accordance with his
theory that Deuteronomy does not ascribe priestly functions to
all Levites. He argues that some had a purely teaching duty to
perform away from the central sanctuary. Such a view cannot
be supported, however, in view of the most straightforward
interpretation of Deut. 18.1-7. See J. A. Emerton, 'Priests and
Levites in Deuteronomy. An Examination of Dr G. E. Wright's
Theory', *VT* 12, 1962, pp. 129-38.

[29] A. H. J. Gunneweg, *Leviten und Priester. Hauptlinien
der Traditionsbildung und Geschichte des israelitisch-jüdischen
Kultpersonals* (FRLANT 89), Göttingen, 1965.

[30] Judg. 17.7 ff.

[31] Ex. 2.1; 6.20; Num. 26.59; Cf. Judg. 18.30; I Chron. 5.29;
23.13.

towns outside Jerusalem, and so would no longer have been able to perform the priestly service of an altar in their old local shrines:

> And if a Levite comes from any of your towns out of all Israel, where he lives—and he may come when he desires— to the place which the Lord will choose, then he may minister in the name of the Lord his God, like all his fellow-Levites who stand to minister there before the Lord (Deut. 18.6-7).

This accords to such Levites the right to come to the central sanctuary, and to perform priestly duties there. The account of Josiah's reform, however, shows that this permission was not granted,[32] presumably because it was unacceptable to the Zadokite priests of Jerusalem. Although Deuteronomy ascribed to all Levites the status of priests, it also recognized that there would be Levites in the provinces who would no longer be able to carry on their priestly duties there. This distinction between the priests of the central sanctuary and the priests of the provinces may not have been an entirely new one, created by the Deuteronomic reform, but have been a distinction which had gradually come into existence.[33] If this were the case, Josiah's reform hardened such a distinction, although it did not create it. The later legislation for Israel's priesthood regarded the Levites as an inferior clergy who could not serve the altar.[34]

[32] II Kings 23.9.

[33] Cf. R. de Vaux, *Ancient Israel*, p. 364, 'Thus a distinction already existed, *de facto* though not *de jure*, between the priests of the large sanctuaries (or, during the attempts at reform, of the sole sanctuary) and the priests in the provinces.'

[34] Ezek. 44.10 ff.; Num. 3.6-9; 8.19; 18.1-7.

In Deuteronomy there is a regulation that the Levitical priests who serve the altar are to live from the revenues of the sacrifices brought to it, and from the firstfruits and firstlings of Israel.[35] The circumstances of the provincial Levites was less satisfactory, and were to be made even more difficult by the Deuteronomic demand for the centralization of the cult. It is for the benefit of these Levites that Deuteronomy places great stress upon the need for charity towards them, and places them alongside the widows and orphans.[36] Thus, although all Levites are regarded as priests, under the surface there is a recognition by the Deuteronomists that inequality existed between those who served the central altar, and those who were in the provinces.

That these Levites had a responsibility for teaching the divine *tōrāh* to Israel has been especially argued by G. von Rad.[37] Deuteronomy itself was a result of this priestly instruction to the laity of Israel. It is significant, therefore, that later passages in Deuteronomy assert that the Deuteronomic *tōrāh* was to be kept in the custody of the Levites,[38] which accords well with the view that these formed the circle from which Deuteronomy emanated. They were thus a gift from God to Israel, which was allied to the law itself. The function of the priests, whom God had given, was not only to serve an altar, but to serve a law. They were teachers and preachers as well as officers of a cult, and in this teaching role they enabled Israel to enter

[35] Deut. 18.3-4.
[36] Deut. 12.12, 18, 19; 14.27, 29; 16.11, 14; 26.11-13.
[37] G. von Rad, *Studies in Deuteronomy*, pp. 13 ff., 66 ff.
[38] Deut. 17.18; 31.9, 24 ff.

the full enjoyment of life before God in the covenant of Horeb.

Throughout Deuteronomy there is a constant emphasis on the debt which Israel owes to God. All its life, both political and religious, is seen to be dependent upon what God has given to Israel. Consequently there is no part of this life which is not a cause for Israel to show gratitude to Yahweh who has made it possible, and it is this gratitude which the Deuteronomists regard as the true basis of worship. The recognition of what God has given passes over necessarily into a response of thankfulness to him, and shows the true meaning of worship. Therefore, in agreement with their theological interpretation of Israel's life as a gift of God, the Deuteronomists show that a particular theological and spiritual meaning attaches to every form of worship.

4

THE MEANING OF WORSHIP

The Incomparable God

THE entire character of Israel's worship, according
to Deuteronomy, was to be dominated by the knowledge that Yahweh the God of Israel was unique. He
was distinct from every other form of god worshipped
by men, and was not to be confused with such non-
Israelite deities. Under no circumstances could he be
set alongside them, to share with them the devotion of
men's hearts, nor could he himself be divided up into
a number of forms, or manifestations, of the one God:

'Hear, O Israel: The Lord our God is one Lord; and
you shall love the Lord your God with all your heart, and
with all your soul, and with all your might' (Deut. 6.4-5).

These words sum up the purpose of worship, and of
life itself, which was set before the citizens of Israel.
Their God could not be identified with any other, nor
could he be honoured by acts of piety imitated from
other religions. He was unique, and the meaning of
the worship of Israel was given to it by the knowledge
of this uniqueness. The harshness with which every
influence from non-Israelite religions was repudiated,

70

even to the extent of demanding the extermination of nations whose religions might corrupt that of Israel, is one of the most startling and revealing aspects of the teaching of Deuteronomy.[1] The undivided God demanded the undivided loyalty of his people's devotion.

The rigorousness of these demands must be set within the context of the religious situation existing in Judah during the eighth and seventh centuries B.C. This is not to excuse the violence of such religious intolerance, but to recognize its true purpose. The pre-Israelite peoples of Canaan, the 'seven nations greater and mightier than Israel', no longer existed as political entities. The descendants of these peoples had long since been absorbed into Israel under the umbrella of the Davidic state. What had happened, however, was that the ancient religious practices of these peoples had survived through that tenacity which makes people reluctant to abandon rituals to which they have long been accustomed. The primary target of the Deuteronomists was not the ancient peoples who had inhabited Canaan, but their venerable cults which had threatened to undermine Israel's faith, and thereby its very existence as the people of Yahweh.

The two basic foundations of the Deuteronomic teaching were that Israel was a people uniquely chosen by God, and that this God was entitled to all their love and gratitude. The belief in Israel's unique destiny had its origin in the belief that the God who had planned and revealed this was unique:

Behold to the Lord your God belong heaven and the heaven of heavens, the earth with all that is in it; yet the

---

[1] Cf. especially Deut. 7.1 ff.; 12.29 ff.

71

Lord set his heart in love upon your fathers and chose their descendants after them, you above all peoples, as at this day. . . . For the Lord your God is God of gods and Lord of lords, the great, the mighty, and the terrible God, who is not partial and takes no bribe (Deut. 10.14, 15, 17).

It is not wholly correct to use the term monotheism for this Deuteronomic doctrine of God. Deuteronomy recognized that other nations worshipped other gods, and the propriety of this worship is not denied.[2] It is intent rather upon denying that Israel can have any other god than Yahweh, because he alone has made Israel what it is. At the same time the superiority of Yahweh to all other gods, both in power and moral worth, is fully asserted. For Israel the practical consequences of monotheism are explicit, although the more abstract conception that only one God exists is not made. The idea that all the various gods worshipped by men are really manifestations of one and the same God—a monotheistic tendency not unknown in the ancient world—was utterly abhorrent to Deuteronomy. This would have robbed Yahweh of that uniqueness which was his, and which had been made evident through his deliverance of Israel and his revelation through Moses. For Israel to have turned aside to the worship of any other god, or to have identified the manifestation of any other god with that of Yahweh, would have been tantamount to selling its birthright among the nations of the world.

In Deuteronomy this theological assertion of the incomparable nature of Israel's God, and the refusal to adopt any alien cultic practice into Israel's worship

[2] Cf. especially Deut. 4.19.

of him, is not a selfish ideological claim, but is given the fullest moral justification. The religion of the pre-Israelite inhabitants of Canaan is described as morally corrupt, and contradicting the most fundamental of human ties and feelings:

When the Lord your God cuts off before you the nations whom you go in to dispossess, and you dispossess them and dwell in their land, take heed that you be not ensnared to follow them, after they have been destroyed before you, and that you do not inquire about their gods, saying, 'How did these nations serve their gods?—that I also may do likewise.' You shall not do so to the Lord your God; for every abominable thing which the Lord hates they have done for their gods; for they even burn their sons and their daughters in the fire to their gods (Deut. 12.29-31).[3]

Deuteronomy was waging no abstract ideological battle over the merits of differing religions, but was involved in a life and death struggle for the maintenance and survival of its own God-given religious insights. The issue at stake was whether Israel could survive as a nation if its religion were no better than that of the nations which it had supplanted. Since its very existence as a nation was attributed to its religious relationship to Yahweh, if this were destroyed could the nation survive? Israel was faced with this searching question in the seventh century B.C., and the severity of the crisis accounts for the sharpness with which the Deuteronomists opposed every form of cult which could find no sanction in their own religious traditions. What was at stake was ultimately the union of morality with religion, and what we find in Deuter-

[3] Cf. Deut. 18.9-14.

onomy is the refusal to accept that God could demand of men, in the name of religion, what the conscience of society condemned as immoral. The strongest affirmation of the uniqueness of Israel's God, and the demand that every Israelite should yield a total allegiance to him, were necessary if the Deuteronomists were to preserve the integrity and moral character of their society. Their religious controversialism was the outcome of a deep moral passion for the welfare of every citizen of the nation which they loved.

The Central Sanctuary

The most interesting of the demands which Deuteronomy introduced in its attempt to combat the threat to its own unique understanding of Yahweh was that which centralized all cult at one single sanctuary:

But you shall seek the place which the Lord your God will choose out of all your tribes to put his name there to tabernacle[4] it; Thither you shall go and bring your burnt offerings and your sacrifices, your tithes and the offering that you present, your votive offerings, your freewill offerings, and the firstlings of your herd and of your flock (Deut. 12.5-6).

There are several significant features of this law of the sanctuary, which represents a considerable elaboration over the earlier law of the altar contained in the Book of the Covenant.[5] Whereas earlier a number of

[4] The Hebrew reads 'for his habitation', but with a slight emendation of the vowels this can better be read as 'to cause it (i.e., the name) to dwell'.

[5] Ex. 20.24-26.

altars had been regarded as permissible to Israel, these were now reduced to one which is described as 'the place which Yahweh your God will choose'. Furthermore it is no longer described as the place to which God himself will come to bless his people (Ex. 20.24), but as the place where he will cause his name to dwell.

We must ask whether any precedent existed in Israel for claiming such a unique status for one sanctuary as the place chosen by God for the receipt of his offerings. It is tempting to look back to the very earliest days of Israel, before the introduction of the monarchy, when Israel was organized as a tribal federation. It has been widely held that during this period the Israelite tribes worshipped at a central sanctuary, or, more precisely, sent representatives to participate in such worship. Thus it has been argued that the Deuteronomic law is the revision of an old custom, deriving from the days prior to the monarchy.[6]

There are certain objections, however, which must be raised against such an attempt to derive the law of cult centralization from the organization of the amphictyony. First of all the cultic organization of Israel in this early period is far from clear, and even those scholars who have accepted that one shrine was given a particular pre-eminence as the place at which the ark was kept, have been forced to assume that this was moved from time to time. Only in this way can the movements of the ark be accounted for, and the importance of several sanctuaries be explained. The evidence that any one sanctuary had a unique im-

[6] Cf. G. E. Wright, 'Deuteronomy', pp. 324, 410 f. G. von Rad, *Deuteronomy. A Commentary*, pp. 16 f.

portance, even for a brief period, is far from clear, as W. H. Irwin has shown.[7]

Furthermore, even ignoring the uncertainties that surround the claim that pre-monarchic Israel had a central sanctuary, it must be objected that what Deuteronomy demands is not a central sanctuary, but a sole sanctuary. This is a far more stringent and significant demand which cannot be derived from the amphictyonic central shrine.[8] The background to this demand for an absolute cult monopoly in Jerusalem must be traced to the unique form of Israelite state religion which had developed in Jerusalem after the building there of the temple by Solomon.[9] Here was a sanctuary with a special claim to pre-eminence because of its particular association with the Davidic dynasty and the doctrine of their divine election to be rulers of all Israel. Therefore, although Deuteronomy does not explicitly state that Jerusalem is the place which Yahweh has chosen, there can be little doubt that this was the case.[10] Jerusalem could not be mentioned explicitly in a document presented as spoken by Moses.

There is a further confirmation of this view in the claim that Yahweh's sanctuary was to be especially chosen by him. The belief in the election by Yahweh

[7] W. H. Irwin, 'Le sanctuaire central israélite avant l'établissement de la monarchie', *RB* 72, 1965, pp. 161-84.

[8] Cf. R. de Vaux, *Ancient Israel*, pp. 336 f.

[9] Cf. my article 'Deuteronomy and the Jerusalem Cult Tradition', *VT* 15, 1965, pp. 301 ff., and the important comments of R. de Vaux, *Ancient Israel*, pp. 327, 339, which I had earlier regrettably overlooked.

[10] Jerusalem is explicitly mentioned as Yahweh's chosen sanctuary by the Deuteronomistic historian. See I Kings 8.15 ff.; 11.36; 14.21; II Kings 21.4, 7.

of the site of the temple is firmly rooted in the ancient Jerusalem tradition.[11]

There is good reason, therefore, for accepting that the law of the centralization of the cult which Deuteronomy presents, was a development of the earlier claim of the Jerusalem temple to be the pre-eminent sanctuary for all Israel. The motive for restricting worship to one single place was in order to maintain the closest vigilance over the operation of the cult, and to ensure its orthodoxy. This conclusion is of particular interest in view of the hypothesis that many features of the Deuteronomic teaching are of North Israelite origin, and certainly do not represent the views of the Zadokite priests of Jerusalem. We must in some way account for the appearance of Deuteronomy in Jerusalem, and explain the enforcement there of its demand for centralization.[12] Fundamentally the reason must lie in the political necessities of the seventh century B.C., after the Northern Kingdom had been swallowed up in the Assyrian empire. Only Jerusalem had retained its strong cultic independence, and its historic claims had undoubtedly risen in prestige subsequent to Sennacherib's failure to capture the city in 701 B.C. There may, however, also have been a strong religious motive, in which the Deuteronomists recognized the value of a single state sanctuary, based upon the old claim to pre-eminence of the Jerusalem temple. If so, it is all the more striking that the Deuteronomists avoided linking this with the Davidic covenant.

[11] Pss. 68.16; 76.2; 78.68; 132.13.
[12] Cf. the views noted in my 'Deuteronomy and the Jerusalem Cult Tradition', pp. 309 f., and see also E. W. Nicholson, *Deuteronomy and Tradition*, pp. 83 ff.

The belief in the election of the Davidic house had previously been most closely related to the belief in the election of Mount Zion.[13]

In this law of the sanctuary we find that, instead of re-echoing the earlier assertion that it would be the place to which Yahweh would come to bless his people, it is described as the place where he would cause his name to dwell. Thus Yahweh's name is introduced as the representative of Yahweh himself. G. von Rad has particularly shown that this represents a theologizing of the older cultic notion of the presence of God in his sanctuary.[14] The earlier view had come to be regarded as too unspiritual, and too prejudicial to the conception of Yahweh's transcendance to be retained by Deuteronomy. More recently R. de Vaux[15] has adduced several significant parallels from Near Eastern sources showing that the setting of one's name in a place established a claim to ownership over it.[16] While it is possible that this legal practice has influenced the formulation of the Deuteronomic doctrine, its immediate background must certainly be traced to the old law of the altar in the Book of the Covenant: 'In every place where I cause my name to be remembered I will come to you and bless you' (Ex. 20.24).

[13] See my *God and Temple*, pp. 49 ff.

[14] G. von Rad, *Studies in Deuteronomy*, pp. 37 ff.

[15] In a review of my *God and Temple* in *RB* 73, 1966, p. 449.

[16] Cf. K. Galling, 'Die Ausrufung des Namens als Rechtsakt in Israel', *ThLZ* 81, 1956, cols. 65-70. H. A. Brongers, 'Die Wendung *bešem jhwh* im Alten Testament, *ZAW* 77, 1965, pp. 1-20.

The reference to the divine name here refers to its cultic proclamation.[17] Such a cultic use was a mode of conveying the blessing of God to the congregation, since the name was charged with divine power, and provided a verbal assurance of the divine presence. It may not, however, have been altogether unconnected with ideas of ownership, since the cult gave expression to the belief that the deity who was present in worship was both the owner of the sanctuary and also of the land upon which the worshippers lived.[18] Thus both the cultic and legal aspects of the use of the divine name may well have been present to the minds of the Deuteronomists. It cannot be accidental, however, that they have avoided adding the divine promise 'I will come to you and bless you'. This is not because they were uninterested in the divine blessing, which is certainly not the case, but because they wished to avoid the idea that God himself was present in the sanctuary. The spiritual and transcendent nature of God, in the Deuteronomic view, precluded his actual presence with his worshippers. Instead that presence was mediated through his name which affirmed his lordship over his sanctuary and people, and conveyed his blessing to them.

The Deuteronomists therefore maintain the ancient Israelite view that the temple is the source of blessing for Israel,[19] but they do so on the basis of a more sublimated conception of the divine nature.

[17] Cf. P. A. H. de Boer, *Gedenken und Gedächtnis in der Welt des Alten Testaments*, Stuttgart, 1962, p. 21.

[18] Cf. Lev. 25.23.

[19] Cf. Ps. 132.13-15:

This advanced theological interpretation of the conception of Yahweh's presence with Israel is also carried over to the ark. In the Deuteronomic injunction for the making of this it is presented simply as a container for the law tablets of the covenant.[20] The earlier notion that it signified Yahweh's presence, and was related to the divine cherubim throne, is completely abandoned. It is impossible to suppose that this was an alternative conception of the ark which had grown up alongside the view which regarded it as a representation of Yahweh's presence. It must be considered as a deliberate attempt to strip the ark of an interpretation which made it the visible expression of the invisible God—an interpretation which was undoubtedly still current in Jerusalem in the time of Josiah's reform. Deuteronomy was opposed to regarding any object as a material link between God and his people. The bond between them was the covenant of Horeb, with its demand for a moral and spiritual obedience to the divine law. Thus every form and furnishing of worship which served to maintain that bond had to be regarded in the light of this spiritual relationship. There was no external or material way

---

For Yahweh has chosen Zion;
  he has desired it for his habitation;
This is my resting place for ever;
  here I will dwell for I have desired it.
I will abundantly bless her provisions;
  I will satisfy her poor with bread.

[20] Deut. 10.1-5. Although this command is perhaps a later addition to the original Deuteronomy, it represents a typically Deuteronomic viewpoint. See E. W. Nicholson, *op. cit.*, pp. 31, 56, 71.

of access to God, but only a personal and spiritual one through loving obedience. This did not render the cult obsolete, but it necessitated that it should be interpreted in terms agreeable to the true nature of God, and of his communion with Israel.

In the light of this spiritual and moralized conception of worship it is important to note that Deuteronomy studiously avoids the assertion that God's setting his name in his sanctuary is 'for ever'. The belief that the divine election of, and dwelling upon, Mount Zion was 'for ever' had been strongly asserted in the cult practised there.[21] Just as they have rejected the notion that the Davidic dynasty had a divine mandate to provide the kings of Israel 'for ever', so also the Deuteronomists oppose the view that Yahweh has chosen his sanctuary 'for ever'. Such an unconditional assertion would, in their view, have obscured the demand for obedience to the law, and would have affirmed a guarantee of the divine favour which ignored its spiritual and moral nature. Already in the tragic fate of the Northern Kingdom of Israel there were exemplary warnings that the cult and its institutions were not in themselves able to save Israel.

The temple of Jerusalem stood as a sign of Israel's election, and had been interpreted as such.[22] The doctrine of election, however, is interpreted by Deuteronomy in relation to the promise to the patriarchs, and its fulfilment is seen in the Horeb covenant with its law. Yahweh's temple is a consequence, but not a guarantee, of that election. Between Yahweh and his people there always stands the law with its demands,

[21] Cf. I Kings 8.12-13; Pss. 68.16; 78.69; 132.14.
[22] Cf. R. de Vaux, *Ancient Israel*, pp. 327 f.

and no cultic or political institution can obviate this fact.

The Worship of the Heart

The personalizing and spiritualizing of worship is a very marked feature of the Deuteronomic teaching. This becomes even more evident in the hortatory discourses which introduce the Code. Here there is a marked stress upon the attitude which the Israelite is to adopt towards God, which quite preponderates over specific injunctions describing how he is to be worshipped. It is the inner disposition to which appeal is made, since the origin of all worship is seen to lie in the hearts of men.

In consequence of this appeal to the inner psychological attitude of worship, two dispositions are especially commanded. These are love to Yahweh, and a continued remembrance of him and his gracious acts towards Israel.

The demand for love to God is set out in such a way as to show the supreme importance which the Deuteronomists attached to it.[23] It represents a new emphasis in Israel, although it was certainly not a new idea.[24] Its appearance in Deuteronomy is fully consonant with the broad appeal made in the book to the underlying motives of religious and ethical behaviour. By demanding the right attitude, its authors sought to secure the right conditions in which Israel would be

[23] Deut. 6.4; 7.9.
[24] Many scholars have connected it with Hosea's emphasis upon Yahweh's love for Israel. See G. von Rad, *Das Gottesvolk im Deuteronomium*, p. 81.

obedient to the law, leading to a fundamental renewal of religious life in the nation.

In a study of this demand, W. L. Moran has suggested that it was influenced by the style and vocabulary of ancient Near Eastern vassal treaties.[25] In these the vassal was sometimes commanded to love his royal superior, thus providing an interesting parallel to the Deuteronomic demand for a love which can be commanded. Thus the comparison of Deuteronomy with these treaties is here carried beyond questions of form and style, and is applied to a vital question of content. The value of Moran's observations and comparisons cannot be discounted, but it must be strongly urged that the Deuteronomic demand for love to God is wholly consonant with the character and aim of the work as a whole. An appeal to a right attitude to God fits closely into the scheme which asserts the spiritual and moral nature of all divine service. It is very questionable, therefore, whether we need to regard the authors as dependent on earlier precedents and analogies for the introduction of such an idea into their work. Certainly it was no mere imitation of an existing covenant formulation, but represents a basic feature of the Deuteronomic desire to awaken a deepened sense of religious obligation. As a result of it Israel's religion was given a warmth and a humanity

[25] W. L. Moran, 'The Ancient Near Eastern Background of the Love of God in Deuteronomy', *CBQ* 25, 1963, pp. 77-87, and the further comments by N. Lohfink, 'Hate and Love in Osee 9, 15', *CBQ* 25, 1963, p. 417, and D. J. McCarthy, 'Notes on the Love of God in Deuteronomy and the Father-Son Relationship between Yahweh and Israel, *CBQ* 27, 1965, pp. 144-7. Cf. also D. J. McCarthy, *Treaty and Covenant*, pp. 118 f.

which it may otherwise never have possessed. It marks an important step in the personalizing of worship, which carried its obligations into the very springs of human behaviour.

The second of the characteristic features of the Deuteronomists' interpretation of Israel's response to God is seen in their demand that Israel should remember Yahweh and his acts of deliverance.[26] We find that the observance of the Feast of Unleavened Bread is given an interpretation which makes it an act of remembrance for the deliverance from Egypt:

And you shall offer the passover sacrifice to the Lord your God, from the flock or the herd, at the place which the Lord shall choose, to make his name dwell there. You shall eat no leavened bread with it; seven days you shall eat it with unleavened bread, the bread of affliction—for you came out of the land of Egypt in hurried flight—that all the days of your life you may remember the day when you came out of the land of Egypt (Deut. 16.2-3).

In a similar way we find that in the motive clauses which the Deuteronomists introduce to certain of the laws there is a command that Israel should remember its own slavery in Egypt and the fact of Yahweh's deliverance.[27] W. Schottroff points out that of the sixteen occurrences of the verb 'to remember' in

[26] Cf. Deut. 5.15; 7.18; 8.2; 9.7; 15.15; 16.3, 12; 24.18, 22; 24.9; 25.17. On this aspect of Deuteronomic teaching see W. Schottroff, *'Gedenken' im Alten Orient und im Alten Testament. Die Wurzel Zakar im semitischen Sprachkreis* (WMANT 15), Neukirchen-Vluyn, 1964, pp. 117 ff. B. S. Childs, *Memory and Tradition in Israel* (SBT 37), London, 1962, pp. 50 ff., P. A. H. de Boer, *op. cit.*, p. 37.

[27] Deut. 15.15; 16.12; 24.18, 22.

Deut. 12 refer to the remembering of past events, especially the deliverance from the slavery of Egypt.[28] There is no doubt that the Deuteronomists intended this remembering of Yahweh's past acts to serve as a means whereby Israel should continue to participate in the redemptive significance of its own history, and to retain a freshness in its sense of gratitude to him, and thus to stimulate that love which was Israel's proper response to his election.

A particular interest of this demand for remembering lies in the question of its background. Much recent study has emphasized the important role of Israel's cult as a means of 'actualizing' or 'contemporizing' past events so that Israel might continue to experience their redemptive significance.[29] In this concern of the cult with past events the vocabulary of remembering was employed[30] so that we may look for some connection between this cultic remembering and the usage of Deuteronomy. It should also be noted that a demand for remembering the gracious acts and attitude of the sovereign is found in some ancient vassal treaties.[31]

Neither the usage of the cult, however, nor that of vassal treaties is sufficient of itself to explain the Deuteronomic demand. There is apparent in Deuter-

[28] W. Schottroff, *op. cit.*, p. 117.

[29] Cf. H. Zirker, *Die kultische Vergegenwärtigung der Vergangenheit in den Psalmen* (BBB 20), Bonn, 1964. C. Westermann, 'Vergegenwärtigung der Geschichte in den Psalmen', *Forschung am Alten Testament. Gesammelte Studien* (Theologische Bücherei 24), Munich, 1964, pp. 306-35.

[30] Cf. H. Zirker, *op. cit.*, pp. 7 ff.

[31] Cf. K. Baltzer, *Das Bundesformular* (WMANT 4) Neukirchen, 1960, p. 93.

onomy an awareness of crisis, and a threat of the
impending disruption of the nation's life, which made
an appeal to remember the nation's origin particularly urgent.[32] The older cultic assurances of Israel's
salvation were placed in jeopardy, and there seems to
be a feeling of loss of identity on the part of the sur-
viving kingdom of Judah. Deuteronomy's strong
demand that Israel should remember Yahweh was an
outcome of this sense of crisis, and an attempt to
ensure that through the reading, teaching and proclamation of the *tōrāh* Israel should identify itself once
again as the people of Yahweh. Through the knowledge of the past Israel would remember its own
election, and so would be made continually aware of
its privileged status, and its continuing debt of gratitude to God. In its demand that Israel should remember, as well as in its demand for a strong personal love
to God, Deuteronomy shows its concern for a spiritual
and theological apprehension of religion.

This is also evident in the Deuteronomic legislation
regarding sacrifices. It is accepted that these have been
demanded by God, and Deuteronomy follows earlier
interpretations in regarding them as gifts offered to
the deity. Yet behind this conception of sacrificial
gifts there undoubtedly lies a crude notion that they
served as the food of God which he required, and by
means of which he participated in the sacrificial ban-
quet at the sanctuary. There is evidence in the Old
Testament that such ideas were at one time current

[32] Cf. G. von Rad, *Old Testament Theology*, I, p. 231, and
B. S. Childs, *op. cit.*, pp. 78 f., 'the concept of memory served a
significant role in Deuteronomy's theology in meeting the crisis
brought about by a reinterpretation of the cult' (p. 79).

in Israel,[33] and we find in the Ugaritic texts several indications that such was the view of sacrifice held in Ugarit.[34] Yet such a crude conception of God, which regarded him as having physical needs which his worshippers were responsible for satisfying, was contrary to the Israelite understanding of his nature.[35] It was particularly offensive to the Deuteronomists, who strongly emphasized the spiritual and transcendent nature of the deity. Thus although they accept that offerings are due to God as his people's tribute to him, they clearly enunciate that this is in order to satisfy the religious need of the worshippers and not the physical need of God:

Before the Lord your God, in the place which he will choose, to make his name dwell there, you shall eat the tithe of your grain, of your wine, and of your oil, and the firstlings of your herd and flock; that you may learn to fear the Lord your God always (Deut. 14.23).

The concluding statement 'that you may learn to fear the Lord your God always' makes it abundantly clear that these gifts of tithes and firstlings were not to be given because God had any physical need of them, but because they were to enable the worshipper to express through giving them a right attitude to

[33] Lev. 21.6, 8; 22.25; Num. 28.2; Ezek. 44.7, 16; Mal. 1.7, 12. The probability is that this was an older popular view which was at one time current in Israel, although R. de Vaux has argued that it was a later intrusion into Israel's religion, stemming from the Babylonian influence during the exile. (*Studies in Old Testament Sacrifice*, Cardiff, 1964, pp. 40 f.)

[34] Cf. W. Herrmann, 'Götterspeise und Göttertrank in Ugarit und Israel', *ZAW* 72, 1960, pp. 205 ff.

[35] Cf. Ps. 50.12-13.

God. Deuteronomy was therefore able to contemplate a situation in which the value of the offerings was converted into cash, and this money spent at the sanctuary on whatever food the offerer desired. This food he then ate in the sanctuary in thanksgiving to God.[36] It was not the gifts themselves which were holy, but the attitude of the offerer, and it is this right attitude of thankfulness that was pleasing to God.

In these revised regulations we see that Deuteronomy is never content simply to preserve the earlier laws of Israel's cult. It is aware that worship has an element of meaning, and it endeavours by interpretation and exhortation to elicit this theological significance belonging to the cult. In the course of this the earlier interpretation of particular rites is revised and refined, and, most of all, the whole cult is set within a context of personal communion with God. The cult becomes an aid to worship, rather than that worship itself, for this latter lies hidden in the secret places of the human heart.

[36] Deut. 14.24 ff.

5

DEUTERONOMY AND THE CANON OF THE OLD TESTAMENT

WE have seen in the foregoing chapters that Deuteronomy is very deeply concerned with the problems of national and religious unity so far as they affected Israel. It stresses that Yahweh is one God, and that in his uniqueness he is not to be confused with other deities. Similarly Israel is one nation, which is everywhere throughout the book treated as a single entity, and which is called upon to make a unanimous response to Yahweh's acts of grace. This insistence on the unity of Israel is all the more significant in view of the appearance of Deuteronomy at a time when the nation had suffered three centuries of division, and when the remnants of the Northern Kingdom had largely been swallowed up in the imperial expansion of Assyria. We have also seen the very distinctive demand of Deuteronomy that Israel should have a completely unified cult at one single sanctuary. Thus the Deuteronomic theology can be summed up as an insistence upon one God, one nation and one cult. These are defined and interpreted through one *tōrāh*, which Deuteronomy claims to be. Thus, although the work points to Israel's unity as a fact, it also seeks to be instrumental in maintaining and affirming this fact. Deuteronomy not only takes a unitary view of the nature of the Israelite tradition, but seeks very consciously to be a unifying interpretation of it.

The Principle of Canonicity

We must understand the importance of Deuteronomy as a religious document in terms of its authors' intention that it should provide a continuing standard of interpretation for the cult which it authorizes, and the covenant which it recalls. This function of Deuteronomy as a standard of faith for Israel is hinted at in an injunction, appended to the original work, which demands that Deuteronomy should be placed beside the ark containing the law tablets.[1] The central object of the cult and the *tōrāh* which interprets that cult belong together.

The very insistence of Deuteronomy that Israel is a unity, and that there is only one legitimate tradition for its religion, suggest that both claims had not obtained full recognition. The appearance of Deuteronomy as a written document was intended to contribute towards the realization of these claims. Before this time Israel had possessed no completely unified and unifying religious tradition. Rather there had existed a number of local religious traditions which shared a measure of common interests and subject matter. In particular there had been a considerable difference between the traditions preserved at the sanctuaries of the old Northern Kingdom, and the

[1] Deut. 31.24-26.

religious and political tradition of Jerusalem. In the latter there was a concern for the Davidic dynasty and for the special pre-eminence of the Jerusalem temple, which was understandably rejected in the North. Here the older memory of the pre-monarchic federation, and its focus on the Horeb-Sinai covenant, were held in greatest esteem.

Deuteronomy set out to provide a single unifying interpretation of Israel's religion,[2] and it intended that this should be acceptable to, and binding upon, all sections of the nation. It has therefore some features which represent a compromise between the various traditions of earlier Israel. While Jerusalem is accepted as the site of the sole legitimate sanctuary for the worship of Yahweh, such acceptance is set within the context of an overall focus on the Mosaic covenant made on Mount Horeb. We have already pointed out how carefully the Davidic covenant is ignored by Deuteronomy, and its unique claims discounted. It is clear that there appeared in Israel with Deuteronomy an explicit claim on the part of one document to present a normative interpretation of Israel's religion. Here for the first time the principle of canonicity was connected to an extended written document which claimed to be binding upon the whole nation. Although it is not wholly appropriate to speak of the book of Deuteronomy being canonized in 621 B.C., its acceptance brought the principle of canonical authority into the open, and gave it a definite focus.

With the acceptance of Deuteronomy as an instrument of reform, canonical authority was placed in a

[2] Cf. G. von Rad, *Old Testament Theology*, I, pp. 225 ff.; II, p. 395.

written document which was used to interpret the cult of Jerusalem. Admittedly the centralization of worship at Jerusalem established a canonical cult as much as a canonical document, since the authority of both was upheld. Nevertheless a religious document came to be regarded as of unique authority, and was allowed to exercise a determinative influence upon Israel's religious development. It was accorded an authoritative status which placed it above the existing religious and political authorities of the time. In this way a written document came to be regarded as of greater authority than either prophet, priest or king, and it is this principle of authority which lies at the heart of any understanding of canonicity. The historic revelation of God's law through Moses was placed above any contemporary disclosure of divine *tōrāh* through cultic personnel. Thus a unique situation of the past was regarded as of greater revelatory significance than the continuing media of revelation through the cult.

This distinction between a revelation of the divine will in the past, and the contemporary declaration of that will through prophet or priest is fundamental to the whole conception of a canonical document. What God has given once and for all stands above every subsequent revelation of his will, even though it does not render these superfluous. It provides a norm by which their own genuineness can be tested. We have noted how Deuteronomy legislates in precisely this way for the prophets (Deut. 13.1-5). The insistence that the prophetic office is none other than the office of Moses (Deut. 18.15-22) must be intended to ensure that the prophecy does not contradict the Mosaic teaching (cf. especially 18.20). Similarly the Levitical priests are regarded as the cult personnel whose primary charge is the *tōrāh* document once and for all given through Moses. They are the servants of a canonical law. The concept of a canonical document, therefore, is derived from the unique authority accorded to the prophetic person of Moses, and from the unique situation in which this document was given to Israel.

Prophecy and the Canon

It has been argued, most recently by R. H. Pfeiffer,[3] that the basic principle of canonical authority is prophetic. The prophet declares his message as a direct word from God, and invokes no secondary authority derived from any religious institution. His word is from God, and its authority is self-authenticating. Pfeiffer argues that such a prophetic authority lies behind the teaching of Deuteronomy, which is presented as the word of God given to Israel through the prophet Moses. Thus Deuteronomy is a prophetic word of God, and is above any kind of institutional authority manifest in Israel's religion. Its authority is derived from the prophets, and claims the same kind of direct authentication from God himself as they do. Thus the idea of canonical authority is regarded as a prophetic characteristic, so that the formation of the Old Testament as a canon of sacred scripture is essen-

---

[3] R. H. Pfeiffer, 'Canon', pp. 501 ff. Pfeiffer argues that Deuteronomy was deeply influenced by the reforming prophets since Amos, and that Josiah and his contemporaries erred in describing it as a book of priestly *tōrāh*, and not as the transcript of an oral prophetic oracle (p. 502b).

tially derived from the prophetic revelation which formed its starting point.[4]

Many scholars besides R. H. Pfeiffer have argued that the teaching of the great eighth-century prophets lies behind Deuteronomy, and has powerfully influenced its authors in their undertaking.[5] It is certainly significant that in this book Moses is presented as a prophet,[6] which thus shows a similar understanding of the great leader's role as does the prophet Hosea.[7] There are certainly points of connection between Deuteronomy and the major prophets of the eighth century B.C. That this influence, however, was direct and immediate, so that we must regard Deuteronomy as an attempt to transform the prophetic utterances into legislation, is certainly mistaken.

Deuteronomy is a priestly–Levitical–work, and this fact seems fully reflected in the way in which Deuteronomy itself regards the Levites as responsible for the preservation and transmission of the book. At a great many points it betrays a far greater interest in the cult and its regulations than we can regard as probable for the disciples of Amos and Hosea. Furthermore we have noticed that, although Deuteronomy is unique among the Old Testament law collections in legislating for prophets, it does so in a way which places its own teaching above them. It associates this

---

[4] Cf. Th. C. Vriezen, *An Outline of Old Testament Theology*, Oxford, 1958, p. 258, 'The Old Testament revelation came to the people of Israel first and foremost through the intermediation of prophets.'

[5] Cf. most recently E. W. Nicholson, *Deuteronomy and Tradition*, pp. 73 ff., 122.

[6] Deut. 18.15.

[7] Hos. 12.13.

94

superiority with the historical figure of Moses, and the connection of its teaching with the covenant between Yahweh and Israel made on Mount Horeb. Deuteronomy does not simply claim to be *tōrāh* in general, but the special *tōrāh* given to Israel in the plains of Moab by Moses on the eve of their entry into the land. The unique authority of Deuteronomy does not lie in its prophetic character, but in its historical connection with Moses and the covenant basis of Israel.

One further point may also be made in arguing that the canonical authority of Deuteronomy cannot be explained as a consequence of the prophetic character of the book. Deuteronomy claims to be *tōrāh*, and we have already seen that such divine instruction belonged to the prophet as well as the priest. When, however, this *tōrāh* is defined as 'testimonies, statutes, and ordinances', it is no longer applicable to the known forms of prophetic address. We must entirely reject Pfeiffer's argument that this 'legal' understanding of Deuteronomy was an unfortunate mistake.[8] Rather it is inseparable from the whole character of Deuteronomy as a covenant document. Even the hortatory sermons of Deuteronomy are a form of address which is not found in the prophets.[9] The authors of Deuteronomy plainly did not regard themselves as prophets, nor seek to present their work in the forms of prophecy. They presented it as derived from the institution of the Horeb covenant with its legal stipulations. While, therefore, there are undoubted re-

[8] See note on p. 93.

[9] Cf. G. von Rad, *Studies in Deuteronomy*, p. 69; 'The Levitical Sermon in I and II Chronicles', *The Problem of the Hexateuch and Other Essays*, p. 268.

lationships between Deuteronomy and the prophets of Israel, this was not a simple relationship but a very complex one. The authors of Deuteronomy were Levites, and their claim to present to Israel a unique statement of the intention and requirements of Yahweh was dependent upon their belief that they derived these from Moses himself, and the covenant which was mediated by him.

In one point, however, we can see that the ability of the prophet to make a direct pronouncement from God did enter very materially into the authority accorded to Deuteronomy as a basis for Josiah's reform. When the genuineness of the newly discovered law book was in doubt, the prophetess Huldah was consulted.[10] She delivered an oracle which attested that the book was genuine, that Israel had previously been unfaithful to its demands, and that Josiah would die in peace, because he had humbled himself before God. The promise of this oracle did not unfortunately prove to be true. Nevertheless, the message of Huldah gave to Deuteronomy the *imprimatur* of prophetic authority, affirming its genuineness and declaring it to be of God. The divine authority of the prophetic word was thereby involved in the recognition of Deuteronomy as divine *tōrāh*, but this was in regard to its authenticity, since it was in its claim to be an authentic revelation of the demands of Yahweh's covenant that its true authority was seen to lie. Its canonical status consisted in its relationship to the covenant, rather than in its prophetic character.

[10] II Kings 22.14-20.

96

The Covenant and the Canon

We can see that, while the prophetic attestation as to its genuineness was important for Deuteronomy, its claim to present a revelation of God's will superior to prophecy derives from its relationship to Moses and the Horeb covenant. It is significant that, although when it was first discovered Deuteronomy was described by Hilkiah the priest as 'the book of *tōrāh*',[11] it is later described as 'the covenant document'.[12] This description fits Deuteronomy excellently, and shows that it is neither a law code in the traditional sense, nor a book of priestly instruction, but a document which sets out the terms and conditions of the covenant between Yahweh and Israel which was made on Mount Horeb. We must ask whether we have in the Old Testament, or elsewhere in the ancient Near East literature, any evidence for the contents of a covenant being written down in extended documentary form.

It is immediately clear that the very earliest Israelite traditions of the Sinai covenant testify that it concerned two tablets of law on which were written the stipulations of the covenant. The contents of these tablets are given in two accounts in the Old Testament, in the first of which the Ethical Decalogue is presented (Ex. 20.2-17), and in the second what has frequently been termed the Ritual Decalogue (Ex. 34.17-26). The historical and literary problems raised by these traditions cannot be dealt with here, but it is important that from the very earliest period of the Sinai covenant's existence, it was accepted that its stipulations were written down on tablets, and pre-

[11] II Kings 22.8. [12] II Kings 23.2.

served for a witness to future generations. Deuteronomy fully accepts this tradition, regarding the Decalogue as the original law of the covenant (Deut. 5.6-21), and giving to it a primary significance. Its own status as a supplementary covenant document is not intended to lead to the replacing of the original law tablets, but to its being set alongside them. Deuteronomy is in effect a supplement to the original covenant law tablets, showing their significance for a wider area of life. As such it is partly based on the Book of the Covenant (Ex. 20.22–23.19), which the Elohist had already linked with the Sinai covenant, even though it certainly did not originate there. When we inquire therefore after the claim of Deuteronomy to present a normative declaration of the will of God for Israel, we can only understand this in the light of the Deuteronomic claim to be a covenant document, and to present in detail the demands which this covenant entailed. Covenant and canon are two inseparably related entities in the Old Testament, and we can only understand the emergence of the canonical principle in Israel, and the formation of a canon of sacred scripture, by reference to the need for a covenant document in which the nature and conditions of the covenant were set out. The institution of a covenant required a permanent witness setting out its origin, purpose and stipulations, so that future generations might know them. The Deuteronomic historian was pointing, therefore, to a very fundamental feature of Josiah's law book when he described it as a covenant document.

The claim that the form of Deuteronomy has been strongly influenced by that of international vassal treaties finds an interesting support in this connection. In a number of Hittite treaties from the second millennium a specific stipulation is included which demands that the covenant document should be preserved carefully, and re-read at regular intervals. Thus the existence of a documetary witness to the covenant, and the provision for its regular re-reading, were intended to exert a controlling influence in the maintenance of the treaty as an institution. This is undoubtedly a closely similar function to that which the authors of Deuteronomy envisaged for their work. It was to be a covenant document, not simply because it described the history and contents of Israel's covenant with Yahweh, but because its preservation and public proclamation were to exercise a controlling influence upon Israel's obedience to that covenant. It was therefore a normative document, and by its presentation of the requirements of the covenant in writing it established a principle of canonicity within Israel's sacred literature. Thus the unique authority of Deuteronomy, which set it above other written documents, and above contemporary divine *tōrōth* through priest or prophet, lay in its form as the document of the covenant which bound Israel to Yahweh. Admittedly such a canonical literature was already in existence in Israel in the two law tablets, but the great advance of Deuteronomy is immediately to be seen in the range and comprehensiveness of the matters with which it deals. From a brief law summary it expanded the covenant document to cover the essential bases of Israel's political and religious life. We must conclude, therefore, that the fact that Deuteronomy established a new form of canonical literature in Israel derives from its relationship to Moses and the Horeb covenant. It declared to Israel the will of Yahweh expressed in that covenant, and its canonical authority derives from the acceptance of a written law setting out the covenant stipulations. Thus the idea of a canon derives from the fact of the covenant, and the need to provide in written form a declaration of what this covenant entailed.

Even if the influence of the vassal-treaty form upon Deuteronomy is questioned, this does not invalidate the argument that the book of Deuteronomy was intended to exercise a role in the covenant between Israel and Yahweh analogous to that of the written document, sealed before witnesses, in political treaties. There is an analogy of function in similar circumstances, which is wholly borne out by the title of 'covenant document' given to Deuteronomy.

In an examination of the role of Deuteronomy as a covenant document N. Lohfink[13] has suggested that there was kept in Jerusalem, for a considerable period prior to Josiah's reign, a covenant document which was revised from time to time. Lohfink argues that Deuteronomy was the form which this had attained by Josiah's time, and thus represents a version of a long-established written tradition. Deuteronomy was therefore of Jerusalem origin, contrary to the widely held scholarly opinion that its real background lay in the Northern Kingdom. This interesting thesis fails to carry conviction because of the lack of any clear evidence for the existence of such a document

[13] N. Lohfink, 'Die Bundesurkunde des Königs Josias. Eine Frage an die Deuteronomiumsforschung', *Biblica* 44, 1963, pp. 261-88, 461-98.

prior to Josiah's time when Deuteronomy was discovered. The theory of the Deuteronomistic historian
that a written law of Moses was handed down through
Joshua and successive monarchs[14] is undoubtedly dependent upon his knowledge of the discovery of Deuteronomy in Josiah's time, and his desire to affirm that
this is the true law of Moses. The prototype of
Deuteronomy as a covenant document is to be found
in the Decalogue, written on two tablets, and preserved in the ark. Since the Elohist had also connected the Book of the Covenant with the covenant
of Sinai the idea of covenant legal documents, setting
out the stipulations which the covenant contained,
was established in Israel from an early period. Deuteronomy is best explained as a development of these
earlier law documents, representing the literary result
of the preaching and reforming activities of Levites.
Undoubtedly in the form in which Josiah received it
the Deuteronomic demands were intended to apply to
Jerusalem, but this does not mean that it was fostered
by the Jerusalem priesthood as the local covenant
document. Its forbears were the Decalogue and the
Book of the Covenant, not an otherwise unknown
covenant document in Jerusalem. Central to an understanding of Deuteronomy, both in its form and the
authority which it claimed to possess, therefore, is the
relationship of Deuteronomy to the Horeb covenant
which it was designed to serve. The authority of Deuteronomy as a literary work was dependent on the
authority which was already regarded as attaching to
the Horeb (Sinai) covenant. Deuteronomy did not
create this authority, but rather derived its own status

[14] Josh. 1.7-8; I Kings 2.3; 11.11, 38; II Kings 17.13-16, 34, 37.

from it. Similarly the authority accorded to Moses as the mediator of divine *tōrāh* was seen to lie in his work as the prophet of the covenant. Thus the principle of authority which underlies the beginning of a canonical scripture in Israel must be traced back to the covenant which that scripture was intended to serve.

The Kingship and the Canon

Authority in religion is always a subject which has many features, for it not only deals with questions of divine revelation and authenticity, but also of effective power of administration. A document can only be authoritative among people who accept its claims. This necessarily raises for us the question of the effective authority through which the claims of Deuteronomy were impressed upon Israel as a whole. In this regard the account of Josiah's reform given in II Kings is intensely interesting, for there is left no doubt that it was Josiah himself who was responsible for pressing through the reform on the basis of the Deuteronomic demands. His authority as king was the power which enforced the reform measures.[15]

We have already noted that, shortly after its discovery, the affirmation of the divine word through the prophetess Huldah was required in order to establish

---

[15] Cf. O. Bächli, *Israel und die Völker. Eine Studie zum Deuteronomium* (ATANT 41), Zürich, 1962, pp. 197 f. Bächli regards Deuteronomy as later than Josiah's reform, and regards the figure of Moses in the book as partly dependent on the role of Josiah in the reform. This conclusion, however, is far from convincing.

the genuineness of Deuteronomy as a document of the Horeb covenant. The acceptance of the prophetess's word, and the reforming activity which ensued on the basis of Deuteronomy, however, were the responsibility of the king. Thus Josiah himself was ultimately responsible for carrying through the reform which bears his name. This direct intervention of the king in the affairs of Israel's cult was certainly not a new factor in the nation's life, but goes back to David's time. The formation of the Israelite state carried with it the recognition that the cult of Yahweh was binding upon the whole nation, and the building of the temple on Mount Zion by Solomon was designed to provide a national shrine for Yahweh. David established some of his own sons as priests,[16] and Solomon was responsible for making Zadok the ruling priest in Jerusalem after the banishment of Abiathar.[17] Thus the claims of the Zadokite priests in Jerusalem were based on royal privilege. The administration of religious affairs was very much under the control of the king, who at one time played a prominent role in the cult. Admittedly there were certain limits to the religious authority exercised by the king, based on what was acceptable to the will of the people as a whole.

In the Northern Kingdom also we find that the kings exercised a controlling influence over the cult of certain sanctuaries, especially Bethel.[18] Overall, however, the kings of Israel were less successful than their Judahite counterparts in uniting the religious and political interests of the state. For most of its history the religious and political centres of the

---

[16] II Sam. 8.18.   [17] I Kings 2.35.
[18] I Kings 12.26 ff.; Amos 7.13.

Northern Kingdom were separate, and deeply rooted religious interests provoked reaction against the monarchy. Even so the political power wielded by the king was a strong factor in the development of the cult and certain of the major shrines. The religious and political authorities needed to attain a real measure of harmony if the nation was to remain stable.

Josiah's action in personally initiating measures for the repair of the Jerusalem temple and subsequently enforcing a reform of the cult on the basis of the book of the law which had been discovered was thus in line with the ancient religious authority of the king. While Deuteronomy based its claim to a unique status on the authority of the Horeb covenant, the effective power which enforced its demands upon all Israel was that of the Jerusalem monarchy. Thus we encounter in Josiah's reform a remarkable convergence of sources of religious authority. The principle of authority vested in the covenant between Yahweh and Israel, the authority of the king over the administration of the cult, and even the immediate authority of the prophetic word, were all involved in conferring upon the book of Deuteronomy a unique status among Israel's religious literature. We may note also that the power of the Zadokite priesthood of Jerusalem was represented in the person of Hilkiah, even though not all the Deuteronomic demands were acceptable to the Zadokites.

The dependence of Deuteronomy upon the royal authority may have been a contributory factor to its failure to achieve any very lasting improvement in Judah's religious life, especially after the tragic death of Josiah. If the authors of the law book were Levites from outside Jerusalem then they were denied the privilege of administering the reforms which they had worked so hard to achieve. Indeed they came to suffer through the very movement they had created, since they never obtained the parity which they sought with the Zadokite priests. Nevertheless their activities continued, as we can see in the further additions and revisions to the book of Deuteronomy, the compilation of the great Deuteronomistic History (Joshua–II Kings), and the Deuteronomistic editing of the prophecies of Jeremiah. All of these activities continued in Jerusalem into the period of the Babylonian exile. The development of the Old Testament canon, however, adhered more closely to the Zadokite traditions as we see in the Holiness Code (Lev. 17-26) and the Priestly Document. The final shape of the pentateuchal *Tōrāh* was dependent very much upon these later works, which follow the Jerusalem–Zadokite, rather than the more specifically Deuteronomic, line. Nevertheless, with Josiah's reform a very important milestone was reached in the formation of an Old Testament canon, and the religion of Israel moved closer towards becoming the religion of a book.

6

DEUTERONOMY AND OLD
TESTAMENT THEOLOGY

DEUTERONOMY has a very special theological interest within the writings of the Old Testament. It stands in a unique position because of its strenuous concern to give a theological interpretation to Israel's cult. It emphasizes the element of meaning which attaches to ritual, and seeks to press home by its exhortations an appreciation of this meaning in the heart of every Israelite. It is also clear that the religious ideas and presuppositions which govern this interpretation of the cult derive from an exalted and consistent understanding of God, and a recognition of the spiritual and personal nature of his communion with man. God is conceived as a transcendent spiritual being, and the communion with him which Israel enjoys is made possible by divine grace disclosed in election and covenant. Deuteronomy stands, therefore, within the Old Testament as a work of major theological importance. In consequence of this it is valuable to consider it in relation to the task of presenting a theology of the Old Testament, and to examine closely certain major problems in the light of this one book.

Theology, Religion and the Old Testament

One of the foremost problems which faces the Old Testament theologian is that of relating such a theology to the phenomenology of Israel's religion. Israel itself did not develop a systematic theology summarizing its religious ideas, and setting out its doctrines of God, man and redemption. If we wish to uncover these beliefs we must do so by carefully sifting the extant documents, by reconstructing the meaning that was attached to symbols and rites, and by thinking our way, as sympathetically as possible, into the minds of Israel's leaders, prophets and writers. It has been widely accepted that a theology of the Old Testament should deal primarily with such religious ideas, and should arrange them into a coherent and consistent whole.[1] The task, therefore, has been one of historical reconstruction, working by a process of inference to lay bare the religious beliefs of ancient Israel.

The value of this pursuit does not need to be defended, and our study of Deuteronomy alone has shown that there is much to be learned from it. It is dubious, however, whether the result of this reconstruction can truly be presented as an Old Testament theology, and whether it does not lead to a measure of distortion of the character of Israelite religion. A reflection on the character of Deuteronomy will suffice to show this. Clearly its authors had clear-cut and impressive views about the nature of God and man, and, if they had wished, they could have written an

[1] Cf. the definition of Old Testament theology given by E. Jacob, *Theology of the Old Testament*, London, 1958, p. 11.

imposing treatise on them. This is not, however, what they did. Instead they presented a revised account of the nature and stipulations of the Horeb covenant, and introduced their distinctive religious ideas incidentally, in interpreting certain cultic and political institutions of Israel. They did this because they regarded these institutions as of first importance, and presented their ideas in relation to them. Thus they were fully aware that Israel's communion with God was mediated through a central sanctuary to which sacrificial gifts were brought, and where Levitical priests officiated. To abstract the ideas from the institutions is to present a very truncated version of the teaching of Deuteronomy. It is possible to argue that it is the ideas which have permanent significance, while the institutions were ephemeral, and can have no meaning for us since they no longer exist. This, however, is to pass a value judgment which would certainly be contested on very convincing grounds. Israel's religion was very much more than its theological ideas, and the elaboration of the latter was pursued only to a very limited extent. If we are to understand Israel's religion we must try to understand its whole phenomenology, in the sense in which this term has been used by G. van der Leeuw.[2] It was not just a religion of ideas, but one of many institutions, symbols and rites. The interpretation of these phenomena varied, even though their central function in the religion was maintained. Thus, for example, we have noted that Deuteronomy gives a markedly new interpretation of the temple, which is quite different

[2] G. van der Leeuw, *Religion in Essence and Manifestation. A Study in Phenomenology*, London, 1938, pp. 671 ff.

from earlier and later interpretations in Israel. Yet Deuteronomy is at one with both earlier and later views in recognizing the importance of the temple as the cultic centre of the covenant between Yahweh and Israel. Its function within the religion is accepted, although the interpretation given to explain this is quite new. Other examples could easily be multiplied. Deuteronomy is an excellent illustration of the fact that Old Testament theology cannot simply be a reconstruction of the religious ideas of ancient Israel. It must be concerned to understand the phenomenology of Israel's religion, and to relate Israel's religious thinking to this.

While it is certainly true that, from its own character as written literature, the Old Testament is particularly concerned with the element of meaning in religion, and with the interpretation of religious rites and symbols, it is certainly not exclusively so. We have noted that Deuteronomy was not concerned simply to be a canonical document, but to establish a centralized (and thereby canonical) cult. We must, therefore, recognize that the Old Testament witnesses to more than the religious ideology of ancient Israel, and a presentation of its theology must take full account of this fact.

Theology and the Canon

Just as we cannot identify Israel's religion with its religious ideas, so too we have learnt to recognize that the Old Testament does not simply offer a descriptive account of that religion. Its literature arose as a remarkable product of its faith, and was intended to fulfil a special role in its continuance. To understand how and why Israelites and Jews venerated their sacred traditions, and gave to certain written accounts of them a canonical status is a major theological task. A theology of the Old Testament must in a very real measure be a study of the origin and development of the literature which it contains.[3] It, therefore, must be a theology of the canon of the Old Testament. The question of the origin and development of its canon of scripture is one of first importance to the study of Judaism, which became a religion of a book, and it is also vital to a Christian understanding of the Old Testament.

In the forefront of modern theological study of the Bible lies the question of the relationship between the two Testaments. This cannot be transmuted simply into a study of the historical relationship between Christianity and Judaism, which is not in doubt.[4] The Old and the New Testaments are literary collections accorded a canonical status, in the former by Jews and Christians, and in the latter by Christians only. What is meant by this canonical status? What is its purpose? How did it originate?

We have pointed out in the preceding chapter the importance of the book of Deuteronomy for a study of the origin of the Old Testament canon, and the significance of Josiah's reform for a knowledge of the historical process which led to the definition of a canon. By establishing a centralized cult Josiah en-

[3] This has been especially advocated by G. von Rad in the two volumes of his *Old Testament Theology*.

[4] Cf. the remarks of F. Hesse, *Das Alte Testament als Buch der Kirche*, Gütersloh, 1966, pp. 7, 24 ff.

forced a monopoly of sacrificial worship in Jerusalem which gave it a definitive significance for the whole nation. The Jerusalem cult tradition became the canon of orthodoxy for Israelites and Jews. This was a far-reaching event which was to lead ultimately to the conclusion that the canonical written tradition was of greater authority than the established centralized cult. Already we see a move in this direction on the part of Deuteronomy, where the *tōrāh* of the covenant is interposed between Yahweh and Israel as the mediating agent of the divine will. The covenant document, rather than the chosen monarchy or the chosen sanctuary, has the pre-eminent role as the testimony to Israel's election. The outcome of this movement was not fully attained until the destruction of the Jerusalem temple in A.D. 70 and the formal recognition, in Judaism, of its scriptures as canonical. At this point Judaism ceased to be the religion of a cult, and became the religion of a book, although for many Jews living outside Jerusalem this had long been the practical reality. The many steps which led along this path cannot be retraced now, but the general direction of movement is clear. Deuteronomy, therefore, can be an instructive guide to an understanding of the significance of the Old Testament as a canon of scripture.

We have seen that Deuteronomy aimed at attaining a uniformity in religious practice which it regarded as a necessity born out of the unity of Israel as Yahweh's people, and the uniqueness of Yahweh as Israel's God. As a document Deuteronomy was a work bent on reform, and concerned to standardize the worship of Yahweh by prohibiting and removing all that it regarded as unorthodox and alien. It was designed to exercise a normative control over the cult, and the faith and conduct of those who made use of it. It was, however, more than this, and its character is not wholly represented if it is regarded solely as a code of laws, declaring what is and what is not consonant with the worship of Yahweh. It is, as we have seen, a covenant document, and first and foremost it declares the historical fact of the covenant bond between Yahweh and Israel. It does this by recalling the history of its institution, and by repeated exhortations to remember the gracious acts of God in giving to Israel its land. Possession of the land becomes almost a sacrament of the covenant. The laws are introduced as Israel's response to the action of God, and Deuteronomy is fully aware that unless Israel recognizes Yahweh's love in its election it cannot obey his laws. Thus it proclaims Yahweh's grace as the origin and purpose of the law.

In this way Deuteronomy fulfils a role greater than that of a guide-book of faith and conduct. It serves to maintain the continuity of Israel's religion by setting before each generation the divine word of election and incorporation into the covenant. Each generation stands before Moses, and hears his word declaring them to be the people of Yahweh. Thus Deuteronomy serves to maintain the covenant by extending its authority over succeeding generations. It upheld the divine election of Israel by proclaiming it as a fact, and by showing its consequences in the life of the nation. As a result the authority of Deuteronomy as a canonical document is inseparable from its relationship to the covenant of Horeb. Covenant and canon belong together, and we can see, in the emergence of canonical scripture in Israel, a form of written testimony to the fact of Israel's election. Whereas earlier the temple and the Davidic monarchy had been regarded as the signs of this election, and as assurances of its continuance, so Deuteronomy augmented these with its written proclamation. In time the written testimony became of greater importance than the cultic and political institutions, and ultimately replaced them. There is, therefore, a genetic relationship between the cult and the canon. Each in its own way served to proclaim and uphold Israel's relationship to God as a covenant people. The beginning of the canon, as we see it in Deuteronomy, sheds a valuable light upon the theological significance of the Old Testament as a whole. As a collection of sacred writings it must be understood as a witness to the election of Israel as the people of Yahweh. The Old Testament is neither a creed, defining the scope of faith, nor a legal handbook, determining permitted areas of conduct, although there is much of a credal and legal nature within it. It thus becomes impossible to evaluate the authority of the Old Testament as sacred scripture in isolation from the prior claim that Israel is God's chosen people. It is from this claim that the Old Testament originated.

Promise and Law

In a further point the book of Deuteronomy serves as an instructive guide to major questions of theology which concern the Old Testament as a whole. Is the Old Testament to be regarded as law or promise?

Such a fundamental question reveals one of the most deeply rooted divergences between traditional Jewish and Christian interpretations of it. Similar differences have arisen within Protestant Christianity, and the Old Testament has been presented as a book of law,[5] or a book of promise.[6] When we turn to Deuteronomy we are faced with a document which has been regarded as one of the central manifestations of law in the Old Testament. Yet it is very far from being a book which ignores, or discounts, the divine promise. On the contrary the promise of its land and nationhood forms the fundamental declaration of Israel's election. The patriarchal covenant, and in fact the whole history of the patriarchs, are interpreted under the general theme of the divine promise. Promise becomes inseparable from election. It would be very misleading, therefore, to identify the legal aspects of Deuteronomy with legalism. The divine promise and the covenant in which it is made manifest are regarded as assured realities which the law does not establish, but which establish the law.

At the same time there is in Deuteronomy a very real awareness that the final goal of Yahweh's promise is yet to be fulfilled.[7] Israel has entered into Yahweh's

---

[5] Cf. for a recent positive presentation of this view G. Wingren, *Creation and Law*, Edinburgh, 1961, pp. 123 ff.

[6] Cf. F. Hesse, *Das Alte Testament als Buch der Kirche*, pp. 67 ff.

[7] Cf. G. von Rad, 'Deuteronomy', *IDB*, I, p. 838a, 'This period also must have regarded itself as still being between the election and the fulfilment of the great promises—i.e., as a generation which, although it had already lived in Canaan for centuries, was nevertheless still waiting for the final fulfilment of Yahweh's promise'.

covenant and received its inheritance, yet it has still not obtained the full enjoyment of Yahweh's purpose. It stands between the promise made to the patriarchs and the full realization of it in its own life. We must guard, therefore, against over-generalizations of 'law' and 'promise' in the Old Testament. Deuteronomy makes it very clear that there is a promise which stands behind the law, and which gives it direction and meaning. Similarly we cannot abstract from the Old Testament a theme of 'promise' without recognizing its relationship to the law which served as a means towards its realization. The relationships between the two become highly complex, and admit of no easy differentiation. The law does not necessarily threaten, or invalidate, the promise, nor does the promise render the law superfluous. Both have an integral place in the Israelite tradition, and both are fully represented in Deuteronomy. We find in this book, therefore, a very instructive guide to the theological character of the Pentateuch as a whole with its dual themes of promise and law. Both find their focus in the covenant to which they are related.

Description and Evaluation

In one last point we may consider the light that Deuteronomy can throw upon the nature of Old Testament theology. Of the major questions of methodology which have arisen in relation to this subject none is more fundamental than the question whether it should be a descriptive discipline or a normative one. Thus K. Stendahl[8] has argued very vigorously that

[8] K. Stendahl, 'Biblical Theology', *IDB*, I, pp. 418 ff.

biblical theology is essentially a descriptive undertaking. This is an extremely attractive position, and one which places it firmly in line with the task of historico-critical exegesis. Over against it we may set the view which argues that biblical theology, because it is theology and not simply a history of religion, must be normative in its method of working.[9]

Both positions can easily be presented as extremes, and no doubt in the actual working out of such a theology a great deal more common ground would be found than might be expected at first. There is a concern with a common subject matter, the contents of which must be studied and expounded as fully and as accurately as possible. How do these methodological questions appear if we set them against the task of writing a theological interpretation of the book of Deuteronomy? If we seek to apply a purely descriptive approach we are struck by a basic preliminary question: What are we to describe? Can we simply enumerate the basic religious ideas which become evident in an examination of Deuteronomy? We have stressed at the very beginning of this study that there is no more consistently theological book than Deuteronomy in the Old Testament. Yet even so we also have had to insist that Deuteronomy is not a theological

[9] Cf. N. W. Porteous, 'The Theology of the Old Testament', *Peake's Commentary on the Bible*, rev. ed. edited by M. Black and H. H. Rowley, Edinburgh and London, 1962, p. 151, 'OT theology has a normative function in respect of which it can claim the right to be regarded as theology'. Cf. also the view of Th. C. Vriezen, *An Outline of Old Testament Theology*, Oxford, 1958, pp. 121 ff., who argues that Old Testament theology finds its starting point in the New Testament revelation.

treatise, but a book of religious instruction, which is presented as the document of Yahweh's covenant with Israel. If we concentrate upon the theological ideas of the work, we are reconstructing the theology of its authors, but this is not the same thing as a theology of Deuteronomy itself, since there is a wider concern in the book than solely with religious ideas. It is vitally related to the institutions of Israel, both political and cultic, and a major part of its purpose is to reform and use these in the interests of a national reawakening of faith and obedience to God. As we pointed out above, there can be no theology of Deuteronomy which is intelligible in isolation from the history of Israelite religion, as we know it in the seventh century B.C. The political and religious institutions cannot be transformed into ideas, nor are we entitled to consider Israel's religious ideas by themselves, and to form them into a coherent theology. A descriptive approach to a literary document such as Deuteronomy must be regarded as belonging to a phenomenology of Israel's religion, rather than as providing us with a set of ideas which we can call a theology of Deuteronomy. This is not to deny the need for such a descriptive approach, but rather to affirm its necessity. There can be no theology of the Old Testament which is not thoroughly conversant with the history of the Israelite-Jewish religion from which it emerged. We must reaffirm what we have already said earlier that a description of Israel's religious ideas, or even of the contents of the Old Testament through which those ideas become known to us, ought not to be regarded as the final province of an Old Testament theology. The descriptive approach, made possible by historico-critical research, leads to a history of Israelite-Jewish religion, and can reveal to us the place which the Old Testament traditions had within this. A theology must go further, and exercise some evaluative function in considering the Old Testament and its religious background. It must go on to compare the various religious ideas found within the Old Testament with each other, and relate them to the function of Israel's cult and its institutions. It must weigh the significance of the Old Testament documents in relation to these ideas and institutions.

In this regard the book of Deuteronomy may be especially instructive. Here is a document which argues in a forceful way that Israel is God's chosen people, and which presents a whole cluster of religious ideas around this doctrine of election. Once we have understood what Deuteronomy has said about this election we must consider it in relation to other conceptions of election in the Old Testament. We must interpret it in relation to those institutions, above all the Jerusalem temple and Davidic monarchy, which served Israel as signs of this election. We can see then how Deuteronomy presents the Mosaic law, expressed in the Decalogue and in Deuteronomy itself, as the true testimony to Israel's status as God's chosen people. The canonical document becomes the reflection in history of a supra-historical fact of the divine will. The canon becomes not merely a norm for faith and conduct, but a testimony to the purpose of God with Israel, and a means of effecting that purpose. It affirms the divine election by bringing succeeding generations of Israelites under its privileges and claims. The book of Deuteronomy thus becomes a divine instrument for

maintaining the continuity of Israel, and for uphold-
ing the divine welfare of those within it. Conceived in
this way the Old Testament canon becomes a living
word of God to succeeding generations of his people,
as well as a source through which we can uncover the
world of faith of ancient Israel. It is the province of
an Old Testament theology to examine these matters,
and to show why the Old Testament emerged as a
collection of writings through which Judaism, and
later the Christian Church, were to become conscious
of themselves as God's chosen people.

We may claim, therefore, that Deuteronomy is a
major theological document of the Old Testament. In
it we have one of the most thoroughgoing attempts on
the part of Israel's religious leaders to attain a clear
theological understanding of their religion It aims at
a maximum theological comprehension of historical
tradition and cultic observance, and it uses theological
comment and interpretation as means for renewing
and reforming faith. It is the textbook of a programme
of religious education which sought to guide Israel
through the political and religious crises of the seventh
century B.C. Its greatness lies, not in the success which
it immediately achieved, but in the new direction
which it gave to Israelite religion. It did not rescue
Israel from the peril of political defeat and ruin, but
it pointed to that realm of faith and of the spirit, where
love and obedience mattered more than passing success or failure.

INDEX OF AUTHORS

INDEX OF BIBLICAL REFERENCES

Index of Biblical References